BIRTHING A LIVING CHURCH

Birthing a Living Church

Virginia Hoffman
Foreword by Dennis Geaney

CROSSROAD • NEW YORK

1988

The Crossroad Publishing Company
370 Lexington Avenue New York, N.Y. 10017

Copyright © 1988 by Virginia Hoffman

Printed in the United States of America

Library of Congress Cataloging-in-Publication Data

Hoffman, Virginia.
  Birthing a living church / Virginia Hoffman: foreword by Dennis
Geaney.
      p.   cm.
  ISBN 0-8245-0900-5
      1. Church renewal—Catholic Church. 2. Catholic Church—United
States—Controversial literature.   United States—Church
history—20th century.   I. Title.
  BX1406.2.H57 1988
  262'.02—dc19   88–18810
                                                              CIP

Portions of chapter 7 are adapted from the author's "Can We Get
There from Here?" an article that appeared in the March 1988 issue
of *Upturn*. Used with permission.

Dedicated with love to

My wise and loving husband Joe
—also to Amy, Rebecca, Joseph, and Stephen—

the 9:45 Family in Round Lake,
the Ministry Center Family,
and all who are bringing church to new birth.

Contents

Part III
Life after Birth

Foreword

The hierarchical church that has served American Catholicism well for over a century, is dead but not buried. Will a new church growing out of the faith of the people come to life? Will the new be born out of the shell of the old, or does there have to be complete disintegration of the old? Virginia Hoffman does not believe that cosmetic changes or new programs will bring the church back to life. In *Birthing a Living Church* she sees the base community model as the womb for the birthing of a church where gospel values are shared as the bread and the cup at a family meal.

The rallying cry of the liturgical movement of which I have been a part since the 1940s has been "the eucharist is the primary and indispensable source of the Christian life." If we could bring the Sunday eucharist to the center of our communal life, we would experience the Second Coming. *Birthing a Living Church* does not disagree, but the book points up a fundamental difference between clerical and lay mentalities. Liturgists are inclined to begin with the altar; lay people begin with life. Many of those sitting in the pews on Sunday are obviously bored, and not aware that the church could be different. Many leave without reflection on why; others have withdrawn emotionally from what is happening at Sunday Mass; others, particularly women, leave in anger.

Birthing a Living Church does not begin with a clerically dominated eucharist but with the "two or three gathered in the name of Jesus." They may be gathered to discuss raising a family, their concern for neighbors or neighborhood, or for refugees from Central America. The community becomes church when the gathering becomes intentional, when it is aware that they are gathered in the name of Jesus Christ. This is the pure New Testament understanding of Christianity. Organization or institution is necessary as order is to a household. However, when the institution through its bureaucratic control system has a stranglehold on the gifts of the members, the church becomes impotent.

Virginia Hoffman comes to the subject as a wife, mother, and teacher who had a traditional Catholic upbringing, but her special contribution is her experience of working with local people to form community outside the traditional parish structure without rejection of the parish. The group uses the resources of the parish, but has its own identity.

However, no movement that is countercultural in a hierarchical church can hope to stay within the household of the faith without theological reflection. This family-centered group opened its own school of theology. Catholic seminaries, which are supported by parish collections, are not open to parishioners, lest the presence of lay people, especially women, interfere with the training of seminarians. The failure of the Catholic Church to make theological education available to the laity is tragic, an example of hierarchical overcontrol.

One of the threads that run through this book is the church's hierarchical control that devitalizes the church. People will not have authority until they claim it for themselves. Clericalism will continue to stalk us until lay people like the Hoffmans and the small cadre of priests and bishops who refuse to follow the party line are in dialogue with each other and willing to risk themselves for the health of the Body of Christ. Catholics across the country are networking as they establish a growing consensus in a vision of a church centered in life rather than in lifeless rituals and decrees. The eucharist will come to life as it did in the Emmaus story in which two disciples showed their care and hospitality to a stranger as they walked with him on the road. The breaking of the bread in the inn was a vision of the Second Coming, which people experience after they care and share. *Birthing a Living Church* offers an example of how we North Americans can approximate the base communities of Latin America where church leadership takes ideas from the poorest of the poor.

This book is not a blueprint. It does not pretend to offer a model that can be duplicated. I hope there are thousands of such efforts across the country by persons who are fired with a vision of what Jesus is calling us to. Virginia Hoffman has the faith and the courage to be a burr under the saddle of church leaders who have no vision. She has not written off the church, because of its tired and outmoded structures; she remains a Catholic because she passionately believes that church can be an effective witness of Jesus Christ in this world. There are not two churches—the house of the clergy and the house of the laity—but a body composed of many members called to function as the one body symbolized in the one bread.

This is an exciting book that could not have been written by a cleric. Its ideas come from a wife, a mother of four children, a theology professor who dialogues with her students, and a member of a grassroots community that maintains a relationship, at times stressful, with its parish church.

Dennis Geaney

Introduction

When I began my theological studies, I would talk with people who were afraid that the church was dying because Latin was gone. Now I am hearing people say we will surely lose the eucharist because the clergy is disappearing. Elements of church structure are showing signs of age—rigidity, brittleness, forgetfulness of its own youth. The old institution is groaning and writhing, and whatever it does only adds to the pain. There is much rushing about and wringing of hands. Some are applying band aids; others are "curing" the symptoms by smothering the patient.

There is a struggle from within, yes, but it is not demonic, as some fear. It is the natural course of things. The covenant God made with Israel has been a constantly renewing source of life. Whenever the pattern of life became old and stiff, whenever attention focused on religious externals in place of fidelity and care, prophets always arose to call the people to new vision, new life.

Like the message of the prophets, the message of Jesus called for new focus, new centering, new life. A community of his followers, seeking that new life, grew within the elder tradition until its own "nutritional requirements" forced a separation and birth.

If we would only learn to see church as a *living* organism, see the simplicity of its vital systems and the power of the Spirit to deliver life—in spite of our every attempt to fossilize it—we would recognize the anguish of this moment too as a birthing. This book is to help in recognizing, supporting, and celebrating the new life.

Birthing a Living Church is for those persons of any Christian tradition who recognize the continuing struggle between legalism and life, who understand that reformation is an ongoing need. Some of the situations described here may no longer be an issue to some denominations, but are still troublesome to Catholics. It is my hope that this book will be particularly affirming to those whose call to ministry arises from God-in-their-lives, a help to those trying to untangle the ordination question, and a hope to those who fear that their struggle toward participatory church may be coming to a dead end. It is one voice in an ongoing dialogue, to suggest and explore a new vision of church.

I want to thank the many friends who have made me more aware of the loving presence of God, and have shared with me the experience of birthing a living church. My children deserve special thanks for suffering patiently with me through the longest "pregnancy" on record. My husband, too, has my heartfelt thanks; he has been my partner and mentor for twenty years as our understanding of church has evolved, and has labored with me over every point expressed here.

I am grateful to Michael Leach at Crossroad Publishing Company, whose enthusiasm allowed this book to come to completion, to Jon Nilson at Loyola, whose suggestions provided welcome assistance in the preparation of the final draft, and to Dennis Geaney, whose comments are a gift of support and encouragement. None of these people is to blame for the faults herein, but what is healthy and good owes much to their midwifery.

V. H.

Part I

Questions Pushing Us toward Birth

1
What—or Who—Is Church?

Since when in the actual Christian experience did it happen that to look for a Church is to look for a living community? *(José Marins and Team,* Basic Ecclesial Communities: the Church from the Roots *[Quezon City, Claretian Publications, 1983], p. 14)*

I grew up in an Irish Catholic neighborhood on the south side of Chicago. Father Kane *was* the church. He is remembered still as a holy and humble man, but there was no doubting that in the square mile that constituted St. John Fisher parish, Fr. Kane was the voice of God. He received that authority from Cardinal Stritch, who received his authority from the pope. And if one couldn't get to the pastor, the two assistant pastors and the dozen or so sisters were acceptable deputies. It was a strong network of authority, the sure source of all the answers straight from the throne of God. If anyone asked "What does *the Church* say about that?" there was no doubt what was meant by "the church."

The bishops began meeting in council—the first such council in a century—while I was in high school. A few of us were given the opportunity to do research on the history of church councils and to present our reports at evening meetings in local parishes. Looking back, I think that experience first began to change my perspective on church.

The people we met were certainly intelligent, successful in their homes and work places, but so helpless within their church. Talk of possible change unnerved them. They had been taught that "the way we do things is the way they've *always* been done." Yet whatever the bishops meeting in Rome should decide to change would be their duty to accept.

Just the study I had done for that assignment had given me a different perspective: that things *do* change over time, that structures and rituals were *not* handed down unchanged from Jesus, and that somehow the *people* are the church. I was angry that no one had ever told us that! My vision was very limited—I knew no church beyond Roman Catholicism—but no longer passive.

If we were church, we were going to have to take a more active role. To do that, we would have to know more than we were hearing in the average Sunday sermon. I started college with the goal of studying theology and working with other adults so we could *be* church, not just passively belong to it.

Our Starting Point

Much of what we had called religion was ethnic culture: a set of habits, old and comfortable rituals, ways of looking at things—all filed under "of course" in our minds. Our "religion" was frequently not so much a choice as a context, already given, out of which our choices were made.

For most of the history of western European Christianity, that context was woven of the warp and woof of divine authority and the political power structure. Often church and government were one and the same. The man with the power might be bishop or prince or both, but he wielded both civil *and* ecclesiastical authority.

The list of rules and taboos for "Christian" Europe was made up of measures to quell this or that religious faction, along with expedients of a civil nature—no matter: it was all one. The original reasons for rules and practices became obscured with time. But the belief that all authority comes from God had fostered the corollary that blind obedience to anyone in authority *guaranteed* one's salvation. Good people did not ask questions; they just obeyed.

We belong to a generation who grew up with "church" meaning male-hierarchical-structure with power to set conditions for eternal salvation. We lived in strict conformity to those rules, with reminders to have no dealings with anyone not "our own." Membership and obedience guaranteed heaven. Members were, for the most part, too grateful for that certainty to threaten it by asking questions . . . until the late 1960s.

Now there seem to be more questions than answers. In the twenty-five years since Vatican II, we have taught children catechism lessons on the *community* we are called to be—and then "graduated" them to an anonymous, lifeless parish. And just as some begin to discover what it means to belong to a community of caring, ministering, co-responsible persons, they come face-to-face with the bureaucracy and manipulation of the institutional church. Too many come to reject "church" altogether as destructive of new life.

We have to disentangle the centuries-old confusion with the word "church."

There is an institution, a structure whose focus and methodology are taken directly from the realm of politics and economics. It has raised armies and demanded allegiance at the point of a sword or threat of economic reprisals. In the United States, institutional Catholicism is acknowledged as one of the most tightly run corporations. But the political and business structure is not the same as *church* in the sense I will use it here, and at times is even at odds with it.

Those who have rejected church-as-regimentation are now searching for something more. Having finally dared to question, we are trying to make the changes needed to allow for a more authentic experience of Christian living. But if we leave behind the authoritarian superstructure in order to get back to basics, will we still have church? It is time to have a deeper look at the original direction Jesus took, to allow our conversion to be complete.

Jesus

If we want to understand the core of the insight Jesus had been given and that he shared with his followers, we have to see that insight in the context of first-century Judaism. Resituating Jesus in his times allows us to hear his message as it challenged the priorities that had crept to the center of Jewish practice. Only then can we recognize that the *same* priorities that Jesus challenged have since moved to the center of Christian life and practice.

Jesus was part of the established religion, the majority, one of a good "church-going" family in a town where nearly everybody went to the same church—like being Lutheran in Minneapolis or Catholic in Chicago. Religious leaders then could command wide respect, and a kind of loyalty made keener by popular hatred of the Roman forces of occupation.

His relatives could point to a covenant on which rested their relationship with God. Originally, the Lord Yahweh promised guidance and protection, and the people promised to worship Yahweh alone and to treat each other with justice. The terms of the covenant were stated simply at first—the ten commandments are thought to have been a concise formula for annual renewal feasts; later on they were augmented to include new insights. By the time the terms of the law were committed to writing, they were already quite complex. By the time of Jesus, the terms covered every element of daily life.

After the exile, there was another dynamic at work here too. The prophets spoke of the call to serve Yahweh, to preserve their worship and tradition so that, through them, God's plan would be achieved. Their care in holding to their tradition would allow that, someday, the whole world would come to worship the one God and live in harmony. The whole world did not have to become Jewish, but those who were Jewish had to carefully protect that identity to be witness, servant, God's instrument for change.

There was an official academy of men who studied the law, interpreted it, debated it, and wrote out all its implications. They had the responsibility of preserving Judaism to serve the coming of the reign of God. Their sense of mission explains their sense of law. Beyond the issues of order, there were layers of practices to preserve and guard that order, layers some people depended on for an inner sense of security or rightness. Their stance was protective, their reasons understandable.

Twenty years ago, the ethics classes in Catholic universities were taught in the same mode. Catholic identity and presence were seen as essential to God's work in the world, so every means was used to preserve and protect that identity. In textbooks any and every moral choice was reduced to a formula: major premise, minor premise, and one absolute and universal conclusion, one *right way* for a *good* Catholic to act in any situation.

The proliferation of laws that fill our nation's legal codes today, covering every possible dispute, would astound the architects of the American Constitution. Human beings tend to nail things down, put it all in black and white, set up something they can point to and be *sure* of. The Pharisees were not *bad* men; they just wanted to be *sure*. And their decisions were the yardstick against which Jesus, his family, his neighbors, were measured.

Jesus was a small-town carpenter with no degree, no credentials to teach. He did not—he could not—begin by demanding an audience. There was no halo, either. He was a working man and a good Jew—his contemporaries would have called him Joshua—and he read scripture and absorbed religious practice in that context. He had the right, like any adult male, to read scripture in synagogue and share his thoughts on the reading; that in itself would not have been unusual.

He observed the common people intimately, and with a compassion that made him aware of inconsistencies between what he saw as the heart of his Jewish faith—social justice and prophetic hope—and the practices he observed. He understood the importance of the law to keep clear the ideals of covenant fidelity to the one God and loyalty to one's people. But the future event that was the reason for preserving tradition, he saw breaking into the here and now. He spoke to the present moment, and called for the mercy and openhandedness that should characterize the day of the Lord, the year of jubilee, the coming kingdom—now.

He openly disagreed with the focus on Sabbath practices and dietary laws. He saw them as a burden. Shouldn't the Sabbath ensure there be one day to rest, to *enjoy* God's creation? Then why should a hungry person *remain* hungry rather than "break" the Sabbath by picking a piece of fruit or an ear of corn? Why should an act of mercy be put off for even a day?

Jewish law had come from a sense of God's speaking to the people in the *present*. But what some legal experts taught was rigid and codified, enshrined the *past*, tried to preserve tradition until God's time in the *future*, and excluded all but an elite few.

Jesus reread the holy books again and again, and spent days walking alone, trying to make the pieces fit, trying to find God again in the muddle of laws and penalties. As he read the scripture, there was one law that superseded all others —direct, simple, to the heart of the matter—the cry of the prophets: make the Lord God the center of your life, and serve, serve, serve your neighbor.

His Vision: Seeds of a New Life

The reign of God, long anticipated by his Jewish ancestors, was the focus of Jesus' vision of how life could be, how life ought to be. The end-time, the peaceable kingdom, the messianic age, begins now—not *after* the emergence of the perfect society, but *as* people begin to live its peace and practice its justice and hospitality. In story after story, he shared the context of his vision: our God is a loving parent who forgives us and cares for us, and invites us to treat those around us as family.

To those whose vision was two-dimensional, Jesus showed a new depth, a new dimension, where we are already related—directly and intimately—to God and each other. Seeing life in that new dimension of relatedness to God made everything take on a new size and shape. Parts of the law that had loomed so ominously over people's lives, able to condemn them as outcast, he saw as relatively minor. And what was so simple, part of Jewish law but not what most would consider "religious practices," Jesus considered to be the heart of it all: if you pass a stranger, beaten and bloody on the side of the road, stop and help him. If you must compete, vie for the lowest place. Share your bread with others. Forgive, not grudgingly, not measuring the wrong, but with an open heart and a warm embrace. Accept each one as your equal. And know that God *loves* you as father and mother, that God is *with you,* and that the reign of God begins *here and now!*

Jesus was a Jew speaking to other Jews. He had no blueprints for a new structure, no rousing speeches to leave the old one. The reign of God was never thought to be contingent on either. Some Roman military personnel and merchants from other trade centers also listened to him. He preached conversion to them all as a *life change* on the deepest level, not a change in one's external religious affiliation.

Jesus said that the word of God is like seed: given fertile ground, it will generate new life. If that is so, then it is no wonder that those who really heard it, who opened themselves and let the ideas penetrate to the deepest part of them, felt something new beginning to stir inside them. Life would never be the same again.

Seeds Generate Community

Jesus did not start another institution. Many of those who followed his vision were good "church-going" Jews who met in homes on a weeknight (Sabbath was Friday/Saturday) to "hash things out," find moral support, care for the poor, share a supper. Those small, home-based communities became a movement *within* an institution that was independent of it and eventually transcended it.

Christianity is *not*, at its heart, an institution. Church, in its most basic form, is a *community* of persons who have heard Jesus' message and been so moved by it that they are willing to refocus their lives, to accept God's gracious love, to receive and support each other as sisters and brothers, and to serve the real needs of others.

Church seems to have always operated best at the level of the *small* community. Members of a church community in the first century knew each other well, became extended family to each other. They knew the strengths of each one—who was best at patching up a quarrel, consoling a widow, getting collected food to the poor. They knew one another's weaknesses, counseled each other, "brought each other home" to their new family.

The communities were in touch with those in other towns, but the experience of church was small, intimate, centered in one's own community and in the household where they met.

In the early days, church was not a power structure. Each household community was a network of *co-responsible* persons: each one had gifts, each was called to use those gifts in ministry, responsibility flowed from ability. Attempts to rank one gift above another or to "lord it over" others were criticized in the writings of the times. The priestly caste of Judaism was repudiated. Only one was to be called father. Only one was recognized as lord and priest and mediator, and all were called to live in a new equality with him and continue to spread his message and his mercy.

The community was the *countercultural* element in town, not the majority; it had no political clout. Like prophets whose actions speak of a deeper reality more central to life, followers of Jesus' vision weighed their decisions against a simpler, clearer set of priorities. They were known to keep company with different nationalities and classes, to go out of their way to care for the poor and homeless, to avoid some patriotic celebrations, and to refuse military service. They called their society to a higher accountability, quietly, by their choices and their lives.

Birthing

Imagine the early Christian community as a young Jewish girl living in her father's house. Her parents honor the traditions of their people and live according to the law. The girl is found to be with child, and the new life growing in her is a source of distress, confusion, pain to her parents. They cannot see that the message and spirit of Jesus have planted the seed of new life in their people again, that God continues in the effort to bring humankind into a covenant of intimacy with the divine. They see only that this pregnancy violates their law.

But the girl senses the wonder of the moment: "when anyone is united to Christ, there is a new world; the old order has gone and a new order has already begun." She is keenly aware of how her child is different from her father's clan, delights in the simplicity and freshness of its childhood, and is careful to nurture her child's uniqueness. We still treasure the stories she wrote of that period, her letters, and the Acts.

The Life Cycle Repeats Itself

But—alas!—too soon the youth was seduced into the ways of the powerful. The small communities, devoted to one another and to Jesus' ministry, became organized, stratified, institutionalized. Christianity came to resemble and even to replace the governmental structure of the waning Roman empire. Worst of all, generations down the line came to know and accept that imperial structure as the *heart* of Christianity.

Structure has become our equivalent of law, a stumbling block as difficult for us to step over as rigid legalism was for our first-century sisters and brothers. Religious identity has become more important than service. Preserving the status quo is more sacred than birthing the future. We are at the same threshold.

Our Moment

Where do we begin to look for church today?

Many who grew up, as I did, with an authoritarian image of church, rejected it as adults, refused any religious affiliation for a period of years, and finally found—or were invited to—a community living a different model of church.

What attracted them to one of these communities was usually a sense of the positive energy of the group: the warm welcome given newcomers; support and care for each other; confidence in their own ideas and abilities, and freedom to use them; willingness to extend themselves—to "be there" for those around them. It was refreshing, inviting and, in the deepest part of themselves, right.

"Love one another: by this shall all know you are my followers." It is this love, this sense of connectedness, among those who walk with Jesus and share his vision and his care and his ministry, that best embodies the original vision: *this is church.* Church is the networking—"family spirit" is a better term—of those who share Jesus' life.

Who, then, has the power to generate church?

The new life that energizes people, motivates them, draws them together, is not to human credit; this is the work of the Spirit. We can sometimes see it, if we are observant enough;

we can welcome it and praise God for it, but we cannot *control* it. The *Spirit* makes church happen. If it is still true that "by their fruits you shall know them," then it is clear that the Spirit is bringing church to birth in many places, without asking the permission of institutions.

Here then is the challenge of church: to live the basics, as Jesus taught them, in community with others. To be church does not mean to wield power, at least not in the wordly, monarchical sense, but taking the lowest place and showing kindness to everyone.

This is the challenge to every new generation. We cannot be content to apply old solutions—force or threats or "pulling rank"—to current problems. True, it is wrong to judge earlier ages by today's insights, and it is difficult to know how they perceived their actions at the time. But we cannot carry around what has become fossilized, worship what has turned to stone. Our God is the God of the living, and each age must seek God in life.

We can no longer afford to look at Jesus' coming as an isolated event that replaced one institution with another. That kept the story at a neat distance, and allowed us to believe that Jesus challenged *them* and never *us*. The criticism Jesus leveled at the first-century school of Pharisees he could as easily direct at elements of twentieth-century Christianity.

We are in a renaissance of scripture now, hearing it as if for the first time, and the word of God *still* has the power to inseminate. All over again, the call to simplicity and service is grabbing the attention of those who had tuned out, generating new life in those who had experienced barrenness. Life stands in sharp contrast to the power play of institutions that rule in Jesus' name.

The question "What is church?" is unavoidable, and for us now the answers beget more questions. How do we act on the knowledge that *we* are church? What kind of certainty does it take to let go of our fossils, to step beyond our taboos?

If we are feeling cramped within institutional forms now, that is good—it is a sign of new life growing again, pushing beyond rigid institutionalization to the greater freedom and greater personal responsibility of the reign of God.

Already many small ministering communities are forming, communities of persons who are mutually supportive and co-responsible, keenly aware of Jesus' presence and his vision, and not afraid to make choices that put them at odds with popular culture or even with institutionalized religion.

We are at another moment of birth. Church is being born—again, as it was the first time—because small groups are sharing the word and allowing it to change their lives. Institutions may follow or they may resist; ultimately it will not matter.

Discussion Questions

1. What did "church" mean to you ten years ago? Does it mean the same today? In what ways is it changing?

2. In what ways are you "feeling cramped" within institutional forms? How does your community experience it?

3. What is your reaction to "church seems to have always operated best at the level of *small* community"?

4. What difference would it make in our religious priorities if we recognized the day of the Lord starting now, and not in the remote future?

2

Isn't Being Church More than Planning Liturgies?

"Which of these three do you think was neighbor to the man who fell into the hands of the robbers?" He answered, "The one who showed him kindness." Jesus said, "Go and do as he did." (Luke 10:36–37)

In the beginning, my center of attention was the act of Sunday worship. Doing it well, I was certain, could create a sense of community and be the catalyst for further involvement. Much of our time together as church community was spent planning liturgies and writing prayers.

Although there is some truth in that approach, we came to see limits to what could be done through liturgical worship.

We had started, like many in our time, from an older view of church. If "church" meant the hierarchical structure, then the activity proper to church—its "ministry"—was the public, or even private, performance of religious rituals. The "right" to do ministry was thought to belong to an elite few. As we came to discover that *we* were church, we made the first changes in that scenario: we would no longer just watch the rituals, we would *do* the rituals and improve the quality of church experience (= worship) for our fellow parishioners. We were reclaiming church by reclaiming our place in its ministry —we thought.

The step was a big one for the times. Liturgy committees were the avant-garde of the late 1960s and well into the 70s. But it was only the beginning. Six persons can spend hours of their week writing so that, on Sunday, another fifty might actively participate in worship. But another three hundred will only sit through the service and fifty more will wonder why it is not yet time to leave. Worst of all, the whole experience of church remained in the sanctuary. During the week that followed, only the original six persons would be consciously aware that they were about the business of being church.

When we made liturgy the central activity of the church community, the only opportunity for involvement was planning or "performing in" the Sunday service. Those who shared that task grew in *their* sense of community with each other; but many, who honestly felt they had nothing to contribute to that work, were left out in the cold. There was so much time and effort spent, but so little growth to show for it. Church was still seen as an elite few; ministry was still limited to ritual.

Those who first hear the call to be church as a call to do ritual, face another question when they realize that ritual isn't enough. What *is* at the heart of the call to be church? As we grow in our sense of what it means to be church, we have to ask ourselves at each step of the way: What, then, is our ministry?

Finding the Roots of Ministry

One of the greatest mistakes in the evolution of Catholic Christianity was what happened to the understanding of ministry. Small communities where all members feel called to use their God-given talents in the service of the real needs of others are no longer the common experience. Instead there is a massive institution in which the organizational tasks, in-house administrative duties, and the performance of rituals lay claim to being primary forms of ministry. A few can "do church"; the rest can only watch. This is *far* from the original understanding. How did it come to this?

Keep in mind that many of the early Christians were *already* part of the dominant religious institution—Judaism. What differentiated them as followers of Jesus was their sense of the immediacy of his presence and *their part* in the ongoing dynamic of his ministry. Every one of them was called to share the good news of God's forgiving love; every one of them was called to feed the hungry, to bind up the wounds of the beaten, to direct the use their own God-given talents to the service of all God's children. Ministry belonged to everyone.

Their Sunday-night prayer and potluck flowed out of their ministries and sense of family. They remembered and celebrated Jesus when they broke bread together, and he was with them because they were *together.* Eucharist belonged to everyone.

The rule of thumb was that *responsibility followed ability,* and everybody had both. Those privileged to have learned the new way from Jesus himself had a gift to be shared, not a prize to keep for themselves. The community of the baptized was church; there were no upper- and lower-class Christians.

In fact, the early followers recognized that intimacy with God and their fellows—hallmarks of Jesus' vision—were markedly different from Judaism. There was no longer any need for mediators to offer sacrifice, no need for a special class who could enter the "holy of holies." Jesus, God's son, was one of *them*; their bodies, temples of God's Spirit; all of them, a priestly people.

The first wave of Christians consciously repudiated any divisions in the new communities that would have been created by their old religious categories:

Leadership ("You must not be called 'rabbi,' for you have one rabbi, and you are all brothers. Do not call any man on earth 'father,' for you have one father and he is in heaven. Nor must you be called 'teacher,' you have one teacher, the messiah. The greatest among you must be your servant"—Mt. 23:8–11);

Cult ("But now Christ has come, high priest of good things which were to be. The tent of his priesthood is a greater and more perfect one, . . . the blood of his sacrifice is his own blood . . . and thus he has entered the sanctuary once and for all and secured an eternal deliverance"—Heb. 9:11–12);

Priestly rank ("You are a chosen race, a royal priesthood, a dedicated nation, and a people claimed by God for his own. . . . You are now the people of God"—1 P. 2:9–10, quoting Ex. 19:5–6);

Nationality, sex, or social status ("There is no such thing as Jew and Greek, slave and freeman, male and female; for you are all one person in Christ Jesus"—Ga. 3:28).

This sense of immediacy and conscious personal involvement were sharpened by the small size of their communities and the intermittent threats of imprisonment and execution that kept their number small. There was a cost; those who made the choice were motivated, committed, ready for a different way of life.

There were, from the beginning, those with gifts for leadership and organizational skills. Elders were elected whose collective wisdom would guide the direction of a particular community. A coordinator or overseer would be delegated by the community or by the elders. There was a team responsible for getting the weekly offerings of food and other necessities to those most in need. At first, leadership came from *within,* and administrators worked side by side with the others in communities where ministry was everyone's call.

A Shift Back to the Old Categories

Anyone who has had to make a change in life patterns—ways of relating to spouse, children, alcohol, food, power—knows that it takes sustained, conscious effort, "one day at a time" over a long time, to make the change a reality. We call it behavior modification when the effort is someone else's; *tough,* when it's our own. Many start out with a burst of energy and a resolve to quit smoking or whatever, but when the plodding becomes painful, find themselves reaching for their favorite brand.

The first wave of Christians was committed to change whatever cultural or religious patterns they had that came in conflict with Jesus' vision. They embraced ministry, equality, intimacy with God in Jesus, with all the energy we associate with a new venture. But it was not long before the old values and old practices began creeping back into their lives.

In the early days, sure of their direction and eager to change, they had stretched the elastic strap of community life all the way out to the horizontal—all equal before the Lord. Then it began to snap back to the vertical. Organizational roles began to assume an importance out of proportion with the rest of the ministries.

This was due in part to the growth in size of the communities—as a group gets bigger, we tend to lose track of the special role of each member—and partly due to human laziness. It is hard to maintain a high level of involvement over an extended period of time. The gifts and ministries of each individual member took a back seat to those of a few "front office" people, then were overlooked completely.

Leisurely suppers, perfectly suited to the bonding of those gathered, began to fade from the scene. Paul banned them at Corinth because the wine-and-cheese set wouldn't share with the peanut-butter-and-jelly crowd. Some other houses settled for pared down meetings to escape notice during persecutions.

But sharing a meal was a value that should never have been permanently eliminated. Did it take us twenty centuries to learn that fast food doesn't satisfy the deeper hunger? Meals gave way to token food; community bonding and encouragement were replaced by cultic ritual not so different from Jewish patterns of worship.

The community coordinator became the usual, then the designated, leader of eucharist. As eucharist evolved from a supper to a religious rite, the coordinator came to be the one with the "power to perform" the rite. In the time the group members spent being together, when they acted out who they were as a community, there was a subtle shift in group consciousness from that of *being* church, a priestly people united in Jesus, to that of *belonging to* a sect governed by cultic authorities.

The Jewish temple sacrifice, which had stood in contrast to the Sunday-night Lord's supper, was brought back as the model of the eucharist. The concept of a mediating priesthood, once seen as having been *replaced* by Jesus, was dusted off and used to describe the role of the overseer (*episkopos*) and, by extension, that of the elders (*presbyteroi*). *Recognized* ministries dwindled down to the "in-house" duties of administration and "performing the sacrifice" of eucharist, and those once empowered *by* the community to coordinate *their* ministries gradually became the ones who *owned* all ministries.

Civil Power

Rome at this time ruled the Mediterranean world, and that rule was anything but secure. European tribes threatened the northern borders, and Asian tribes were moving into Europe from the east. Rome needed soldiers to send to the front, and needed to consolidate the empire at home.

Part of the traditional patriotic fervor was the myth of the divinity of the emperor, though few gave it credence anymore. Burning incense was like saluting the flag, a gesture of loyalty. Christians considered it all idolatry and refused to go along with any of the patriotic festivals. The idea of killing people in war was equally abhorrent, so Christians refused military service. They were regarded by some as eccentric, by others as traitors to the empire. Periodic campaigns to force compliance by economic pressure, jailings, or executions had little effect.

Constantine (early fourth century) was shrewd enough or desperate enough to try another approach. Claiming to have had a vision of a cross (a known Christian symbol) and the rising sun (revered by sun-worshipers as well as by Christians), he rallied disparate factions to his ranks. Christians were granted the right of free and open assembly in the empire—and a place in the army!

This is the point at which the inner stratification of Christian communities—the existence of a governing stratum charged with organization and the performance of cult—merged with the power structure of the. empire. Bishops, chosen by their respective communities for their natural leadership ability, gradually expanded their role to fill the void of middle management in the empire. Filling the place of the old aristocracy, bishops were given land by the government and expected to maintain order in provincial towns. No longer were Christians the small, prophetic communities whose lives and actions challenged society's customs. Now they *were* the society, the government.

Throughout the fourth century, Christianity was given more privileges and other religious groups more constraints. Theodosius, Constantine's successor in the late fourth century, made a decision that sealed the transition. He made it mandatory that all in the empire espouse the Christian religion.

Notice it was no longer a matter of becoming one with a small family of Spirit-energized persons, but of subscribing to a pattern of rules and rituals in order to unite the empire. By the end of the fourth century, Christianity had ceased being a persecuted minority and had become instead the dominant majority, exercising its own economic and political constraints against all other forms of religion. (Theodosius also relinquished the title of *pontifex maximus,* high priest of the Roman polytheistic worship, a political/religious title later claimed by the bishop of Rome.)

The Bottom Line

No longer were all the baptized called and commissioned to continue Jesus' ministry. Now that baptism was devalued to *passive* membership, *active* ministry shifted to those called and commissioned by ordination. The concept of Christian ministry had gone from the washing of feet to the exercise of power, from the responsibility of all to the domain of a few.

The movement from the streets back to the sanctuary, and from the sanctuary to the imperial mansion, was a tragic distortion of the original vision. Lost on the way was the sense of intimacy with God so central to Jesus' humanity, the family spirit among his followers, and the universal call of *all* Jesus' followers to ministry.

The rise of early monasticism was, in some ways, a response to the rise to power. Those really devoted to a simple God-centered life found themselves in a rapidly growing body of less motivated members and a more wordly set of priorities. From the beginning of the period of civil power, when everyone became Christian and Christian meant less personal investment, those who wanted to follow the gospel did not just follow the program. Some went to the desert.

During the centuries that followed, there have been other notable attempts to let go of power and status, and serve the poor—Francis of Assisi and the Beguins, communities of charitable women. Nevertheless, the main line of development of the leadership structure continued to grow in the direction of power. Less and less responsibility was in the hands of the baptized, more and more in the hands of the clergy and hierarchy, thus firmly establishing the two-tiered—authoritarian and passive—church.

What Now?

We, too, have found the dead ends. We used to think we would be doing the primary act of church—ministry—if we managed to penetrate the exclusive domain of liturgy and parish administration. Through prayer, study, perseverance, and professional work without pay, a number of pioneers attained posts as liturgists, youth ministers, and even (a few) parish administrators.

But from some of those who "made it" to the inner circle, came the insight that moving *inward* does not bring one closer to true Christian ministry, but can instead leave one trapped and isolated inside a large bureaucracy. Some are opting out of the bureaucracy for a life of grassroots ministry, closer to the call of the gospel and closer to those in need.

Another venture in the search for ministry—the activity of those who are church—came about with the recent renewal movement. Those who met in homes began to discover in those small gatherings some of the earlier sense of church. The use of prepackaged renewal programs had the potential to move the perceived base of active ministry from the rectory to every home—but without follow-up, has managed only to leave it in limbo. Parish staffs put the whole burden on the programs. In many places, participants were brought right to the brink—*talking* about the call to ministry as part of the call to full Christian living—but stopped short of taking the next step. Instead they looped into another round of discussions.

Those who pursued their quest beyond the dead ends found their way out of the labyrinth by following the sense that the early Christians had of ministry. They took their direction from Jesus' own way of life and the stories he told.

When asked for directions to the center of life, Jesus told the story of the good Samaritan. Since then, many of us have followed the Samaritan home. The story does not point to worship: those associated with religious ritual were the ones who passed by. It was a story of an outsider, whose people had committed unforgivable compromises vis-à-vis "the right form" of worship, but who knew in his heart what God called him to do.

Ministry is *service*, tending to the *real* needs of *real* people. Ministry is *presence*, giving our focused attention to others so that we can feel their needs as keenly as our own. Service and presence together is *primary* Christian ministry. This clear, "new" awareness stands in contrast to the very limited ways we used "ministry" before.

The responsibility for ministry belongs to all. Basic to living with Jesus in baptism is the conversion of each one's own gifts to the service of others. We are *all* called to use *whatever* gifts each of us has, and our time and attention, to heal the *real* hurts and feed the *real* hunger of those around us.

The role of the community in all this is to create a base— a place where bonding happens and God's presence is felt, where we can come home to those who are family to us, and a place from which we can go forth refreshed and ready to serve. What we do when we gather as a community—our celebration of eucharist—should support and encourage and restore one another for this ongoing ministry of service.

Liturgy functions best when it flows *from* other ministries. When we made it our focus, too often Christian community life began and ended there. When we let go for a while, put less time into liturgy meetings and channeled our time and efforts into service ministries and community building, our celebration of eucharist took on a new depth we had not known before. The ritual signs of liturgy should be based on, made real by, a wide range of front-line ministries and deepening relationships. Breaking bread should sign a supportive community.

If all members are using their gifts in service and helping others to do the same, many ministries will thrive and church will be vibrant and alive. Ministry will, again, belong to everyone.

Centuries of Christians were taught that "official" church ministry was primarily ritual, and that ritual was primarily someone else's domain. That was an unfortunate misunderstanding that crept in by the fourth century, but one we can no longer blindly accept. Neither can we stop halfway to our goal, and settle for putting more people with more "official" titles in ever bigger offices. It is not enough to point to a wider class of "owners" if the rest still see themselves in a role of passive inactivity.

We can no longer settle for lovely liturgical performances, staged by a committee of designated liturgical ministers, while those in the pews remain anonymous and isolated. Our time together should be spent actively engaging each other, recognizing God in our midst, not just generically, but incarnated in the crowd of faces waiting to be recognized on Sunday morning. We need to find the place where worship and ministry meet: serving God and each other with our attentive presence, becoming community/family to each other and with Jesus, and together reaching out to touch the rest of our neighbors so they will feel the warmth of God's love as well.

We know we are called to be church. But we will search in vain for ministry at the heart of that call until and unless we chart our course by the first markings Jesus gave us, until we set our sites past palaces and cathedrals to the simple people in sandals carrying bread.

Discussion Questions

1. How does the concept of ministry presented in this chapter differ from others you have heard or held?

2. Have you experienced this: "a few can 'do church'; the rest can only watch"?

3. What does "ministry belongs to everyone" say to you? To your community?

4. Have you been to a Samaritan's home? What was it like? What was he or she like?

3

Must Ministry Be
Dependent on Power?

When Jesus had finished this discourse the people were astounded at his teaching; unlike their own teachers he taught with a note of authority. (Matthew 7:28–29)

Now as they observed the boldness of Peter and John, and noted that they were untrained laymen, they began to wonder, then recognized them as former companions of Jesus. (Acts 4:13)

From Paul, an apostle, not by human commission, but by commission from Jesus Christ and from God who . . . chose to reveal his Son to me and through me, in order that I might proclaim him among the gentiles. When that happened, without consulting any human being, without going up to Jerusalem to see those who were apostles before me, I went off at once to Arabia, and afterwards returned to Damascus. (Galatians 1:1, 15–17)

There are pockets of Christians all over the country who have made the commitment to active ministry: in soup kitchens, shelters for the homeless, centers for peace and justice, and the less organized, often unseen acts that model the good Samaritan. But many others who have the same understanding of ministry cannot take action. Why? They are still waiting for the power.

What happens when we confuse ministry with power? People become intimidated. They hesitate to use their gifts without permission from someone else. "Father said he doesn't see a need for that." "The bishop said this isn't the right time." "We can't just have people going around *doing* things; there has to be some control!"

"Power" becomes the narrow bend in the river where a thousand people's gifts can be logjammed by one person's lack of vision, the constriction in the artery where oxygen-bearing blood is held back.

What else happens? Others are given responsibilities for ministries for which they lack the necessary talents—chosen in preference to those who *do* have the gifts—because "they have the power." They operate mechanically. They may keep a parish functioning minimally, like a patient on life support systems, but they deprive the local community of all but a vegetative existence.

Why are ministry and "power" at such odds? To answer that question, we need to look at the nature of ministry, differentiate between empowerment for ministry and institutional control, and measure the cost of the damage done if one is used in place of the other.

The Nature of Ministry

Ministry is caring for the needs of another in the context of God's own larger and ongoing act of loving care. It is *real* service that *anyone* can recognize, but flows from a relationship some might not see. Ministry reaches out to all God's children to heal them and help them grow, to bring them to wholeness and to bring them together. It is part of the ongoing work of creation, a construction zone in today's world. Ministry is a creative act.

Empowerment vs. Control

Ministry flows from the life and work we share with Jesus. The same Spirit that energizes Jesus also gives us the power— and the responsibility, and the energy—to do ministry. And we receive from our communities the affirmation of our gifts and the confidence to use them. All who are baptized into Jesus are *empowered*—by the Spirit and by the community—to use their gifts in ministry.

On the other hand, we saw in Chapter 2 how the merger of a segment of the Christian population with the power structure of a dying empire took place. What was born of that union was the political salvation of Europe: it restored order, established lines of control, became the ultimate authority in temporal as well as spiritual matters, and served the people's needs. After many centuries of development, power and control have become dominant characteristics of institutional Christianity. That is not to say that, along the way, there were not prophets, individuals who resisted the power model and chose alternative ways to live their Christianity. But leadership moved in a fairly consistent direction toward power.

To get back to the simplicity of the gospel call, some twentieth-century Christians are having to work around an authoritarian institution with its own priorities—structure, ritual, an "empowered class"—and its own rules, to perpetuate the structure at any cost, to control ritual, and to maintain distance between classes.

So what happens when we try to discern the direction of our next ministry? We can ask: Is there truly a need here? Do I have the necessary gifts? Is there some affirmation for this among the members of my Christian family? This is discerning the Spirit; through this process we come to true *empowerment* for ministry.

Or, we can ask the institution. Any decisions made by the institution will be based on its own priorities: Will this make

the power structure less secure? Will control over any assemblies be maintained? Will this clearly delineate the province of
those with "power"? This is *not* empowerment but control: it
stops more ministry than it energizes.

"Power," used in this sense, is like a tourniquet on a healthy
arm; it stops real ministry, dams the flow of life.

The Cost of the Damage

What we have produced by identifying ministry with power
is a huge mausoleum where the original dream of a community, living with Jesus and sharing his ministry, lies buried.
What we continue to hand on, instead of a living and growing
dynamic community, is an edifice where all is rigid and dead,
where all the roles are defined—everyone entombed on their
proper shelf—and there are no surprises.

Take Alicea. For years she wanted to start a ministry to her
area's growing Spanish-speaking community. She asked her
pastor's permission. And each time she asked, he had more
"reasons" why there was no need or why it would not work.
Instead of working among the people, she was still on her
shelf, busy devising new ways to convince the pastor.

Bob wanted to start Bible study meetings; the person he
asked wanted another program started. Bob is now running
that person's program. No one is doing Bible study.

A friend who has been trying to move into more active,
person-to-person ministry told me recently, "I want to give
'their church' back to the priests. They keep putting huge piles
of bricks in my way when I want to do something. According
to them, if it's not a rite that happens in a church building, it
just doesn't count." The cost of that "power" is measured in
services lost.

Several individuals from different church communities were
regularly visiting patients and their families in a local hospital.
Sometimes, especially during holidays, there might be six vis-

itors there one day, and no one the next. They wanted to coordinate their own efforts and those of other volunteers so someone would always be available. But no one dared to act because, supposedly, such ministry was "owned" by the closest parish. They had no "power."

Cooperation and generosity are held hostage to "power": "Whose program is it?" "Who has authorized this?" "Who is going to get the credit?" Some Catholics would never give to a Baptist relief effort; some Protestants would never support anything done by Catholics. And some within the power structure would rather ministry go undone than relinquish control by encouraging independent efforts.

Then there are the men in the deacon program, some of whom were off the mausoleum shelf for a time, becoming more active in their communities, but are finding the "formation" program aimed at making them better (quieter) shelf material. If a class is poorly taught, a waste of time, there are no options. If a trainee chooses not to suffer in silence, his loyalty is questioned.

They tell themselves, if we are quiet, if we do not make waves, if we do as we are told, then one day we will be given "the power." What kinds of ministry will they do then? If they graduate "fully formed," they will do only what their superior sees and permits. Will *they* be more empowered? Will the community be better served?

Titles are *not* real power—hunger doesn't see rank, just bread—but they can get in the way of a lot of real ministry.

To guard the distance between those who have "power" and those who do not, the institution has insisted on the practice of celibacy. From early on, candidates for officialdom are taught that loneliness is next to godliness. All socialization is kept among the ranks. This creates a number of other ills.

A cleric once told me that, as a group, priests "never talk with each other about our own spirituality, or about anything deeply personal. It is only women who have given me permission to do that." Yet people hungry for intimacy are sent to the very ones taught isolation. A divorced woman told a group: "The ones who are hurting *don't* 'go to church,' because they feel even *more* alone there. A priest can spot a hurting woman a mile away, and he turns and walks in the other direction."

It takes so much energy—individual and institutional—to maintain the isolation, to guard the "power." That is energy spent that could be spent in service. And the isolation it buys only makes official ministry weaker.

Another cost of the use of "power" is the loss of those who try to escape it. When someone who has received official designation decides that celibacy is *not* essential to using his gifts in ministry, he is expected to petition Rome for release from the clerical state and permission to marry. The request itself takes the form of a psycho-sexual biography, inviting the petitioner to document that he was not completely free to accept ordination in the first place because of a history of sexual license.

Conditions accompany his release: he must move out of the community where he has been known as a priest; he may not teach theology at the college level without the permission of the local bishop; he may not participate in parish worship as a reader of scripture, communion minister, or the like; he may not have anyone present at his wedding save his bride, two witnesses, and the officiating cleric; and finally, he may not *tell* anyone about the nature of this process.

In most cases, the dire measures are only a private humiliation, and they are not always enforced. Bishops and pastors will often choose "not to notice" that professors or involved parishioners are acting beyond their canonical rights. The same administrators, unfortunately, have *not* chosen to risk their "power" to try to *change* such an unjust system.

The men are often alienated by the process, whether they finish it or give it up in disgust. But—here comes the double bind—if they do not ask, they may be blacklisted and prevented from teaching or doing other work within the sphere controlled by the institution.

"Power" repeatedly tries to eliminate the most gifted, the most creative, the most committed to the gospel—those who dare to challenge the structure, even indirectly, when it gets in the way of truth, or building church community, or ministering to those in need.

Do you remember the story of Galileo? He was condemned by Rome in the seventeenth century, forbidden to teach his views, and sentenced to house arrest for saying that the earth revolves around the sun, not vice versa (if Jesus came to earth, then earth must be the center!). Recently, three hundred years after the fact, Rome again issued a statement on Galileo. It still would not say that the judgment was a mistake, only that officials were reopening his case!

It was ironic that shortly after we read the news about Galileo, we heard Inquisitors condemn Hans Küng and strip him of permission to teach. Some say Küng's greatest crime was suggesting that Christianity does not revolve around Rome. Since then Leonardo Boff, Charles Curran, Raymond Hunthausen have been squeezed; the tourniquet is being twisted tighter.

In an age when we desperately need to reexamine Christian practice in the light of the original vision and to integrate our more recent insights, "power" tries to cut off some of those most gifted for that endeavor. In open discussion and debate, ideas will stand or fall on their relative merit. To hear only approved voices is to limit the input to what one person—or a few—can understand, to limit the growth to what one person—or a few—can generate.

The Guarantor of "Power"

For generations, the term "apostolic succession" has been wielded to suppress any questioning or dissent, proof positive that what the institution dictates would be Jesus' choice as well.

But the power of the hierarchical structure, like that of the Pharisaic code, dissipates in the light of the original vision.

Though it is possible to name all the bishops of Rome, there is no consistency in the way they used the title. The earliest were just local leaders who would not think of pulling rank on anyone else. Some were good persons, but some along the way were ambitious, greedy, willing to eliminate any opposition by any means. Some were scoundrels, and others were the corporate heads of what was once Europe's most powerful giant.

On the other hand, if it were possible to trace the *spirit* of Jesus and his earliest followers, we would have a different list altogether. Many whose names are forgotten kept the original spirit of small, ministering communities alive in their own time and place. If we want to establish Christian authenticity, we should ask who is doing that now.

Here in the United States, Abe Lincoln is remembered for his earthiness, his understanding of others, his tireless sense of purpose. If we would want to find another Abe today, would it make any sense to seek out the person who has catalogued Abe's old law practice, or has bought his desk or inherited his name? Or had we better look for the women and men who grace our lives with those same gifts and spirit?

What is happening? Some with "power" are squeezing the life out of the institution. Others may quietly express their dismay, but will not risk their own power to stop it or act on a different premise.

People with the talent, energy, and insight into the needs of their neighbors—gifts that *God* has given them—are beating their heads against brick walls, trying to convince someone with "power" to see what they already see and to give them permission to act.

Meanwhile, the energy that should be spent in caring for the hungry poor is spent—wasted—playing institutional politics, making sure that no one acts without permission, and stifling those who do. We are standing in front of a thirsting world, pouring cups of water into the sand.

Is the "power" controlled by a few the only access to God? Or is the claim to power archaic, counter-productive, a mistake that has lasted too long? One side tightens the stranglehold. The other moves toward greater independence. Each action widens the distance. Each push is closer to birth.

Discussion Questions

1. How has your understanding of "church power" changed since you were a child?

2. In what ways has this chapter clarified the question for you?

3. Describe any incident you know where ministry-as-service was at odds with the "power" structure.

4. Think of some member of the clergy you have admired. What are the qualities you have most admired in that person? If Christianity had evolved differently and there were no power structure, if that person had had no title, wouldn't you still seek out that person because of his or her empathy and "original spirit"?

5. "Many whose names are forgotten kept the original spirit of small, ministering communities alive in their own time and place. If we want to establish Christian authenticity, we should ask who is doing that now." Who do you know, besides members of the clergy, who was or is keeping that "original spirit" alive in your community?

4

Does It Have to Be This Way?

With us, therefore, worldly standards have ceased to count in our estimate of any man. Even if once they counted in our understanding of Christ, they do so now no longer. When anyone is united in Christ, there is a new world. The old order has gone, and a new order has begun. (2 Corinthians 5:16–17)

Does the structure of the church have to be as it is in order to be church? That was the subject of chapter 1, and we came to the conclusion that it does *not*. Christianity is *not*, at its heart, an institution. Church, in its most basic form, is a *community* of persons who have heard Jesus' message and been so moved by it that they are willing to refocus their lives, to accept God's gracious love, to receive and support each other as sisters and brothers, and to serve the real needs of others.

That is what we need to be church; anything else is a matter of comfort, security, or power. If the additional baggage gets in the way of the central elements of church, then it is both permissible and responsible to cut back to something more basic. No, structure does not have to be the way it is.

What difference does it make if we grant that the structure does not have to be this way? Given the fact that it is this way now, do *we* have to conform, or else give up any experience of church? Do *we* have to tolerate it or leave? Does our role have to be this way?

Chapter 2 looked at that question and noted that some Christians are already moving past passivity, past discussion-group Christianity, even past administrative roles in the institution. They are recognizing that *they* are responsible for using their own gifts to care for the real needs of the real persons around them. They are taking ownership of their own call to minister, and they are acting in response to that call. Their lives give witness to the fact that *we* do not have to accept a constrictive role either.

There may be a few brave ones, but aren't most of us caught in the status quo? Don't we have to wait until someone with power, someone "up there," acts to change the system before we can experience any of this? The point of chapter 3 was that all who are baptized into Jesus are empowered—by the Spirit and the community—to use their gifts in ministry. That *is* "the system," though it is different from what we saw when we were growing up.

The Spirit is here, has always been here, empowering us: "when anyone is united with Christ, there is a new world; the old order is gone, and a new order has already begun" (2 Co. 5:17).

The greater part of what it means to be church is what we do in the streets and homes and marketplace—in our availability to be a friend and to give service. When we see a situation that we recognize as a need, that is our call to ministry. Many such ministries are done on the spot. We were commissioned in baptism to do Jesus' work; we do not need additional permission when the situation arises.

Time for a New Beginning

Every organization goes through three stages in its evolution. First, there is a dream, a vision of how things could be, how they ought to be. This original vision energizes a small group of people to devote their efforts to its realization. Along the way, they decide that they will have to institute a few simple structures, just for the sake of protecting and handing on this vision. In time, the structures grow and themselves become the focus of the group.

Some groups dead-end here. The dream is forgotten, and all they have to hand on to newcomers is a rigid structure and the conviction that to challenge the structure *in any way* is to threaten the very life of the institution. College fraternities work that way. Marriages work that way. Every grouping of humans seems to follow the pattern.

The only way out of the trap is by revisioning: getting in touch with the dream that gave birth to the group in the first place, and letting go of whatever structures, traditions, or habits are no longer compatible with it.

How to Get Started

There is a scene in the movie *The Karate Kid* where the wise, old Mr. Miyagi is teaching Daniel how to sculpt a bonsai tree. The boy is afraid to touch the rough-looking plant in front of him, sure he will ruin it rather than transform it. Miyagi shares his secret:

> Close eye. Trust. Concentrate.
> Think only *tree*.
> Make a perfect picture, down to last pine needle.
> Wipe mind clean, everything but tree.
> Nothing exists whole world, only tree.
> You got it? Open eye. Remember picture?
> Make like picture; just trust picture.
> (from *The Karate Kid*, Robert Mark Kamen)

"Make a perfect picture." Then look at what you have, and trim.

Jesus could look at the religious patterns of his own culture and see something simpler within it. We can too. And when the picture is clear enough, it will allow for the letting go—the trimming out—of all the rest.

The branches of structure, control, and status have grown wild since the time of Constantine. To change their shape has seemed so great and complicated a task; many have abandoned their attempts. The possibility for change has been stalled by the inability to imagine church *beyond* what is physically there.

Start with a New Picture

The secret is to start with a *picture,* a vision of church as Jesus described it and lived it with his friends, a vision of the first communities that tried to live his dream. "Make a perfect picture, down to last pine needle."

That is why there is such a hunger for scripture study today —people are trying to reclaim the original vision. It is becoming urgent to know *what* Jesus noticed and *what* he chose to comment on in his own culture, to know where *his* vision of community life stood in contrast to the more formal, institutionalized Pharisaism.

For generations before Jesus, Jews had been anticipating the coming of the kingdom, the reign of God. For some, the image was military and political, full of power and glory, a dynasty like the great kings David and Solomon. Others, like the prophet Jeremiah, looked for a time when humankind would be intimately bound to God by a covenant written on the human heart. For the legal experts of Jesus' time, the celebration of God's reign would be brought about by perfect observance of the law.

Jesus had his own metaphor for God's time, for the accomplishment of God's design, and that was the big feast to which everyone was welcome. He told the story of the householder who prepared the feast and brought in everyone from the streets when those originally invited were too busy to come.

If we "unpack" the parable of the feast, we can find the characteristics at the heart of Jesus' vision of the kingdom:

open-armed welcome to all, even society's rejects, hospitality, a tone of joyous celebration, a sense of equality, willingness to share with all, love, gratitude, . . . The list goes on. Other stories Jesus told reveal more of his vision. The story of the prodigal son (or prodigal father) adds complete forgiveness; the loaves and fishes and the widow's mite—willingness to share one's little with others; the good Samaritan—caring service for all. The possibility of powerful faith, of healing and wholeness and hope, runs through many of the stories. Dick Westley, author of *Redemptive Intimacy,* often refers to the kingdom as "Jesus' dream" for all of humankind.

The core of Jesus' description of the kingdom is in two laws of the Torah: "Listen, Israel: Yahweh our God is the one, the only Yahweh. You must love Yahweh with all your heart, with all your soul, with all your strength" (Dt. 6:4–5, Jerusalem Bible). The other is: "You must love your neighbor as yourself. I am Yahweh" (Lv. 19:18, Jerusalem Bible). He called them the most important laws in the Torah. In the name of those laws, he often violated his own denominational practice as interpreted by the Pharisees.

Jesus did not preach that Jews should leave Judaism, but repeated the prophets' urging to keep the center in the center and move in the direction of the kingdom. He did not instruct Romans to join with his band, but to turn their hearts toward God and others, and move in the direction of the kingdom.

Jesus encouraged his listeners to do two things to build the kingdom: *see* what it should be, and *live the vision.* What does that take? It takes a clear sense of what Jesus saw, courage, awareness of God's love and one's own worth, and support in terms of a conscious connection with God and with others who share the vision.

Is the Kingdom a Denomination?

The kingdom is God's hope for mutual love and service among sisters and brothers. Nowhere, in all Jesus says about the kingdom, does he suggest that the kingdom is available prepackaged. He offered insight, a recipe, a sense of direction. And he made a promise: wherever two or three persons gather in his name—live this way—he will be there with them. From Jesus' words and practice, his vision of the kingdom clearly transcends *any* denomination.

Then, in Jesus' vision of things, what is the relationship between the kingdom and any denominational group? Communities are called to keep the vision clear—keep the center in the center—by *living* it. They need to embody both the outward-directed qualities of service and respect, and the community-building characteristics of nurture and support. Religious communities of every denomination are called to build the kingdom.

Which takes priority—the denomination or the kingdom? Clearly, from Jesus' own example, the kingdom comes first.

If we keep that vision—if we keep the center in the center— then we will measure our communities against the yardstick of the kingdom, not the other way around. We will ask of various communities: Does this group live kingdom? Do they treat one another with equal respect, as befits members of a community? Do they put service to the needs of others first? Is it clear that they have those priorities and are working toward them in a healthy way? Do they nurture and support me, and help me keep the priorities of the kingdom first in my own life?

If we keep that vision—if we keep the center in the center— then we will measure *our own* investment of time and talent against the yardstick of the kingdom, too. The greatest personal investment of our imagination and energies should go to the building up of the kingdom—direct person-touching-person service—*not* to the building up of any one denomination with the hopes that someday *it* will touch the masses.

The vision is becoming clearer: simplicity of life, mutuality, and service stand out as priorities. In the ranking of those things we value most as Christians, these have risen to the top.

Some things that seemed so important years ago now take their places far down the list.

The reordering of values, based on a new/old vision of church, influences every decision we make. Just as each snip transforms the ragged bush into the boy's perfect picture of his bonzai, so each decision we make gives shape to the emerging—living—church.

How Powerful is the Vision?

There are doctors caring for children who use visioning as a method of promoting healing. The child spends time with a therapist each day, drawing the broken bone or whatever, and imagining it mending. It is a means of focusing the body's own healing energies on the wound.

In the treatment of adults, even cancer patients, mental attitude is critically important. Sometimes people survive when the only thing in their favor is their will to live.

On the other hand, we all know people who have "decided" to die—an old person whose spouse has died, or whose friends are all gone—and the body just followed the decision of the mind.

I saw a book in a bookstore a few years ago, David Campbell's *If You Don't Know Where You're Going, You'll Probably End Up Somewhere Else* (Allen, Texas: Argus, 1974). The title was so striking that it helped me clarify my own direction. Then I started quoting it to my classes. Finally I went back and bought the book; I thought the author deserved the price for the title alone.

What really caught my attention was recognizing that the converse of the title is also true. If you *know* where you're going, you *will* get there. If we focus our mind and our imagination and our psychic energies on a goal, we will begin to recognize—first in our minds, then in our decisions, and finally in the world we are creating—the emergence of something new.

A New Order has Already Begun

No, it does not have to be this way. Christian men and women across the country have, for some time now, experienced a new sense of church growing within us and within our communities. We are nourishing that vision with scripture study, the experience of community living, and an awareness of the Spirit in our midst.

At times this growing life within us has been the cause of much discomfort and uneasiness, doubts and fears. We have spoken in vague terms and hushed tones. But now we are in a happier time of certainty and eager anticipation.

At the 1985 conference of the National Association for Lay Ministry (NALM) in San Antonio, I shared this awareness in a homily I entitled "Pregnant." A colleague told me then, after the homily, "It's time we put away the bulky sweaters and put on the maternity clothes and stop pretending." He was right.

For the 1986 NALM conference in St. Paul, we focused on the theme of birthing. Each year when we gather there is new growth to celebrate. The poet Emily Griffin told the assembly she could see the baby crowning—beginning to be born—already.

The last day of that conference, a sweet woman in her sixties sat next to me. We barely had time to introduce ourselves before the speaker began. A few minutes into the presentation she leaned over and said, "Do you know who's going to preside at eucharist this morning?" I whispered "yes." "Why does one of *them* always have to be in charge?! In our women's prayer group back home we do it ourselves and it's much better!" Some are past the crowning.

A vision of the present, in the light of the original dream, allows the letting go of structure, control, and status, in favor of simplicity, mutuality, and service. And once we begin to head in the direction of the light, birth becomes inevitable.

There are still things we have to learn. Much we will have to learn as we go, as did the early bearers of the dream and every parent who has ever lived. We are together in the greatest enterprise we can undertake: we are giving birth to new life, to our future—to church.

Discussion Questions

1. Share with your group your understanding of the original vision of church.

2. "If additional baggage gets in the way of the central elements of church, then it is both permissible and responsible to cut back to something more basic." Keeping your vision central, where would you start to trim?

3. "What takes priority—the denomination or the kingdom?" What do you think? What are the implications of putting kingdom first?

Part II

Can We Get There from Here?
A Birthing Primer

Even for those who are convinced that the time is right for a rebirth of church, there are doubts. Can we get there from here? It is difficult to find the way when so many of our ideas of church are muddled with legalism and institutional protocol.

There is hope: others have made this passage before us. To the extent that we keep our focus, share our experiences with one another, and listen to the Spirit, we will be moving toward the light. We will be moving toward birth.

It would be ideal to be able to sit together around a table, share some food and some ideas, and witness to the guiding power of the Spirit in our lives. Part II is part of that conversation, making available the experiences of some who have already begun the journey, networking through the printed word. Pass the bread.

5

Generating Life

You are, I know, eager for gifts of the Spirit; then aspire above all to excel in those which build up the church. (1 Corinthians 14:12)

Church does not just happen in a room full of anonymous strangers. In order for life to begin there must be a seed. And in many cases that seed is the experience of the *personal presence* of others in community. Those who have had that experience at some time identify *that* as church, and continue to look for it.

A young woman in our community said she and her husband worshiped with a number of parishes, all of which seemed fine to her. But her husband kept looking for something more. When he found a community that, to him, was *living church*— caring and ministering—he knew he had come home. He had found what one blessed experience had told him was possible. And she was introduced to an experience of church she had not known was there.

But there is no guarantee that one will ever find, ready-made, an active, committed, mutually responsible, witnessing and ministering community within twenty miles in any direction of home. So those who are aware of what church *can* be, who have searched for a community and come back tired, are left with a question more difficult than the search: Is there any way we can plant the seed where we are?

If we are going to get "there" (an active, committed, mutually responsible, witnessing and ministering community) from "here" (the all-too-typical experience of large, cold, anonymous, and apathetic gatherings), we have to find a way to plant the seed of community life.

Our focal point in this endeavor is a community of people bonded with each other, who share a commitment to a common faith and to service born of that faith. That is our goal. Traditional Judeo-Christian theology would call that a covenant community; contemporary liberation theology calls it a base community. No matter what name we use, we are called to be family.

Start Right Here . . .

We start with what we have—any gathering of people. It may be a group of people who already know each other and shared some conversations or activities, or it may be an anonymous Sunday assembly. Since many take part in regularly meeting Sunday worship services, and since many have expressed anguish over the bland and distant atmosphere/flavor of those gatherings, that will be our starting place. But it should be understood that these ideas can be applied to other kinds of groups as well.

. . . And Move toward Forming a Base Community

Assemblies are ready-made opportunities for community-building. Most people have a fairly consistent pattern of weekend activities. If worship is part of that pattern, it is usually the same service. If work schedules or other activities sometimes interfere, they tend to find a regular alternate. Those who meet for eucharist at 10 A.M. are usually the same ones.

Most often, though, these worshipers have little sense of bonding with the "familiar strangers" they see each Sunday. They may assume a common set of values, but probably have very little sense of collective responsibility for ministering to others in the area. If we can join with others to introduce family spirit and personal recognition, we can plant seeds of life in even the most barren Sunday assembly.

Food First

One of the easiest and surest ways to begin to form bonds among those gathered is with food. How ironic that Jesus' choice for this kind of gathering was a family feast—Passover seder—and yet the present form of that "feast" is so minimized that we never do experience, during our eucharist, any of the bonding that comes from sharing food. So our first step toward community is to reinstate the sharing of food when Christians gather.

One of the first introductions newcomers have to our community is the cake-and-coffee, juice-and-cookies gathering that follows every Sunday eucharist. Families take turns bringing goodies, plugging in the coffeepot before eucharist, cleaning up afterward. The children play, run around, build friendships. The grown-ups catch up on news, debate weightier issues, arrange for a team to help someone move to a different house. The food says this is "family time," half an hour or an hour and a half, set aside for bonding, enjoying each other's company, building community.

Out of this seed comes the life of our community. Once people know each other, there develops a mutual concern for one another. News is exchanged about someone who is sick or looking for a job. Outgrown clothing is passed down from one family to another. Help is there for "sorting out life."

Community Life Feeds Liturgy

The fact that this group meets every week means that those who gather for eucharist are getting to *know* each other and are growing in that family spirit. That causes changes in the eucharist celebration itself.

In Catholic parishes it is not uncommon to have four or five services every weekend. In many parishes, it is standard procedure to name a fixed group of scripture readers and ministers of communion, and to assign those individuals to perform their duties by rotating them through the entire list of services. This week Sam reads at 8:30, next week at 10. His wife gives communion at 8:30 this week, but next week she is listed for the noon service. Which group is their community?

The members of our community are together every Sunday. Today Tom and Mary will read; next week they listen to Jean and Bud. The person giving you communion might have been the same one who helped you through a problem last week, or baked the cake you will soon be enjoying. Connections become clearer: liturgical celebrations are not performed by strangers, separate from life. We celebrate Jesus among us with the very people who make us most aware of his presence all week and all year.

There are no ushers or altar servers at our service. We wanted our gestures to sign the sense of family we share—that we are not watching a performance but are all personally involved. Families take turns coming a few minutes early to "set up": put the books and cups in place, light a thick, home-style candle on the altar, place a card table near the door where arriving worshipers can put an offering and a piece of communion bread in the appropriate baskets.

After the readings and homily, during the part that corresponds to the Jewish seder meal, all are invited to come forward around the table for the eucharistic prayer. We hold hands when we pray to "Our Father," walk around and share hugs of peace, and receive communion there before returning to our seats.

I can remember theologian Bernard Cooke saying that if the members of a congregation do not have some sense of family by the time they pray to their one Father, they are doing something wrong. For a long time I wondered if impersonal gatherings were unavoidable, standard parish fare. But standing around the altar with our community, making eye contact with so many others who are part of my life, brings joy and peace and an awareness of our call to be family.

What Are We Telling the Children?

The next question we asked concerned the children's level of awareness and active participation. Many families had come looking for something more meaningful to offer their children than "Shh!," "Be quiet!," and "Sit up straight!"

Some adults volunteered to prepare a special presentation of the gospel story so that young children could understand and appreciate it. Songs and a craft project were added so that the message was coming through on many levels. The children rejoined their parents in the main room after the homily, in time to gather around the altar for the eucharist.

This ministry has varied over the years with the changing number of available volunteers. When it began, we offered a Liturgy of the Word for children on the last Sunday of every month. There were separate gatherings for school-age children and for preschoolers. For a while, there was even a nursery for infants—a blessing and a wonder for us but standard operating procedure in many congregations. Right now, we have only preschool lessons, but patient and generous adults are preparing and giving them more often.

Celebrations Worthy of the Name

For special occasions, families will work together to prepare a special evening celebration that will bring home the meaning of some Christian feast. Last year during lent, we shared a simple supper and watched a gospel story enacted by several of our children. The keeper of the vineyard found three young "trees": one with arms outstretched and holding two apples, another lifted branches holding two oranges, the third without fruit. The caretaker tended the barren tree by giving it a big hug. The tree responded with a smile and two bananas. Then we had soup and bread . . . and fruit.

Easter morning, we meet at 5 o'clock in our jeans and heavy jackets to celebrate Jesus' rising. Easter in northern Illinois can bring particularly nasty weather, but that does not daunt our spirits. The time we met in a cold rain—and it is dark as night at 5 A.M. in March—my husband used it to help us understand how the apostles felt, huddled together in the upper room.

We make peace with each person as we begin; "I'm sorry for the time. . . . " It is even more comforting when it comes with a hug. This year, Mary and Joe had us pound our open hands on the ground and notice how dirty they got, like we get in another sense when we pound on people. They had a big stone pickling jar filled with blessedly warm water so we could wash our hands and offer them in friendship to one another.

We sing and tell the stories of how God has delivered us. We light the fire of Jesus' new life, and tell how the eggs and flowers and bonnets also speak of new life. And then we sing some more.

When we finish, we move inside where Tom organizes the team preparing eggs and juice and bagels. We share a single round loaf of bread with our hot breakfast in the joy of the risen Lord.

We still come back for the Roman service, but it pales in comparison with the faith experience we shared before dawn.

Shared Ministry

I am convinced that any effort at community-building where the experience of community is the whole objective is doomed to failure. We close in on ourselves. If we are not getting warm strokes all the time, we stop trying. Rosemary Haughton of Wellspring House in Glouchester and Mary Schramm of St. Martin's Table in Minneapolis—people I greatly admire for their willingness to give and serve—both told me the same thing, and it is consistent with our experience at home. The only way community can succeed is for individuals to be bound together by their common dedication to a common ministry.

When it seemed that we had gone as far as we could go, when internal energies were beginning to run afoul of each other, we took the next step—a big step in terms of growth—to turn our energies outward.

That effort was a project we called "shared ministry" (detailed in the next chapter). We used the homily time on six consecutive Sundays to allow the 9:45 community to come alive as ministering Christians. It challenged us; it changed our outlook. We are co-responsible for carrying the Lord's caring words and healing touch to our weekday world.

Our time together is time to find our center and our energy/ Spirit; but the life of a Christian community, like the life of a good marriage or the life of a growing child, is a balance between venturing out and coming home, between working/ giving and being restored. We are called to be family to each other, and to gradually extend the love and warmth of that family by reaching out to serve others. We are still discovering that unless we do both, we do not do either well.

Discussion Questions

1. How does food add to a gathering? Share a story of a time you have experienced it.

2. How many individuals in your congregation do you know well? Would you feel comfortable confiding in them or asking them for help?

3. What could you do so that they feel comfortable confiding in *you* or asking you for help?

4. What other kinds of experiences might we share that would develop our sense of being family with each other?

6

Internal Development: The Rise of Indigenous Leadership

Jesus' originality does not lie in his spiritualization of the kingdom, but rather in the fact that he saw the true fulfillment of its earthy hopes in a more radical way than many of his contemporaries. . . . Jesus seeks to model, in his own life, a new concept of leadership based on service to others, even unto death. This is the model that he wishes to impart to his followers. In the new community based on the life of service to others, the lust for domination will be overcome at its source. (Rosemary Radford Ruether, To Change the World *[New York: Crossroad, 1985], p. 15)*

Our parish was coming toward the end of a three-year parish renewal program. We had been meeting in each others' homes, engaging in weekly discussions on what it means to live as Christians. Some of us came to the point where we were ready to move into action, but the discussion booklets were not geared to that. So we approached the clerical staff with a proposition.

The outcome of the two meetings in the rectory was that, for each of the six weeks of renewal in October and November, we would use the homily time (of our own gathering only) to make a presentation and lead a discussion that would allow the group to move past talking and make a commitment to some kind of action. We called it "shared ministry."

Shared Ministry: How to Shift Gears from Talk to Action

Most people worship at the same time most weekends. Once there is an experience of community, as we have had, participants make a point of being present with their new friends regularly. Nevertheless, we announced the upcoming shared ministry for two weeks beforehand and asked all to commit themselves to being there for the whole six-week series.

The presentations had to be scripted and given to the clerics to deliver—the perennial issue of "power" again. At the time, however, we were grateful for the accommodations we were given, and we were not about to challenge the conditions.

It would be possible, too, for a community to do this process after worship, at a coffee hour, or at a series of home meetings. Where there's a will, there's a way.

Step One: Introduce a New Sense of Church

We started with a quick history of Christianity. Many adults grew up with the idea that the Christian experience was uniform for all individuals living at any time in its two thousand years of history. It is important to allow them to step back and see it all in perspective.

We focused on four key periods. In the first century, communities were small, intimate. Each person was expected to use his or her gifts in ministry. Church was the whole community of the baptized. Although some were respected for the intensity of their experience of Jesus, there was no ordained clergy per se.

In the fourth century, Christianity entered its period of civil power. Organizational leaders stepped into the void left by the waning Roman empire. Christianity became the official religion of the empire; political and economic pressures were imposed on those who did *not* join.

This second-period shift comes as a surprise to many. It begins to dawn on them that what followed was a matter of human choice, not divine command.

The third period in the spotlight is the sixteenth century. The popular image of God was distant and demanding, enthroned in glory, with Jesus—now Christ the King—at his right hand. Fear of God brought dread of punishment after death. By then, institutional Christianity had the power of a mighty empire—and power corrupts. We addressed the sale of indulgences, the printing of the Bible, the movement toward reform.

Then we looked at our own times in perspective, the impact of recent scripture studies, and current efforts to recapture the original vision.

The object of this quick trip through history is to allow everyone to see the pattern of past choices, and the choices that are ours to make now. We are called to *be* church, to live in the company of Jesus, risen and among us, and to continue his loving ministry to all God's children.

Step Two: Inventory the Local Ministry Needs

The biggest problem with institutional service is that it is often self-serving. The needs it meets are primarily in-house needs. So to take this second step, we addressed that point. Then we took a good look at the parable of the good Samaritan to gain a more basic view of ministry.

Finally we looked at the needs of our area: What kinds of help do our neighbors need? One after another, suggestions were made and we wrote them on a chalkboard brought in for the process.

Step Three: Set Goals for a Specific Period

"What is most needed?" "What are we able to do first?" We began to prioritize, to select some goals for immediate attention and action.

The exhilaration of seeing our ideas and work make a difference spurred us on to pursue the other goals as the first were accomplished.

It is critical that the group decide on its own goals. It ensures teamwork and support in the accomplishment of those goals. It also gives them a real taste of church founded on adult co-responsibility, rather that the passive participation they have known in the past.

Step Four: Discern Each Other's Gifts

This was probably the most beautiful and moving part of the process. It was an opportunity for us to affirm one another's talents and give them more courage to use them. This process may be done with the whole group together only if the group is small or if there is plenty of time to focus on each one. Usually it works best if the group is asked to form smaller groups of five or six, and if everyone in each small group knows the others.

There are many ways to procede, but his seemed to work best for us. Each person is given an index card on which to write their own name (Pat) and one talent that they feel they have. Pass cards to the right; each person adds another gift that Pat has shown. When the cards have gone all around the circle, the last person to the left of Pat reads aloud the list of gifts. It is most convincing to Pat if the others will then tell of incidents in which they saw Pat using the gift they wrote. Then Pat can keep the card for future encouragement.

Step Five: Divide Tasks and Responsibilities

Start with a prayer acknowledging that this is the Lord's work; we will each do a part to help. Then, working from the list of priorities and the talents of the group, try to match the jobs to the talents. It is important to avoid put-downs, and to emphasize strengths. Point out where this or that talent would really be an asset. Set up teams whenever possible for encouragement and support.

Set a date when all participants in the group ministries will come together to report progress, ask for help, and the like. Regular meetings keep it clear that each is accountable to the group as a whole, and also that the whole team is there to help if help is needed.

Some members of a community will not be able to become involved in one of the group's coordinated ministries. It is important that those individuals discern some task, even something they are already doing, that they will hold as their ministry.

Step Six: Commissioning

Once the ministries were decided, we had commissioning. We recited together a statement of commitment, each filling in our name and particular ministry. Then a number of persons from within the group are selected to do the commissioning. They laid hands on each person and said: "In the name of Jesus and this community, you are commissioned to use your talents for this ministry of _____ ('building church' or whatever the particular ministry is)."

Council of Elders

Our focus was shifted outward—ministry had become a household word—and we were concentrating less on who-did-what in worship. Still, we knew that the effort would not last unless some would serve the community itself, sustaining and nourishing our commitment, making us aware of new ministry needs, generally watching over the direction of the community.

So on that Sunday when each person committed individual gifts to ministry in the home, workplace, or town, nine members took as their own a ministry to the community itself.

They became our council of elders and, as their biblical name suggests, they facilitated ministry for the community. They kept clear our focus on ministry and sounded the call when someone needed help. They initiated weekly collections of canned goods and clothing, and asked deacons (in the original sense) to distribute them. They widely delegated the "in-house stuff" so we could be freer to bring Christ to the world. They ensured that our celebrations sign and sustain both our sense of community and our ministries.

We found that it is possible to make use of the natural leadership of a community be reinstating the New Testament council of elders *without* its later cultic dimension. The Greek word for elder, *presbyteros,* has an entirely different and unfortunate connotation now because the original role of the elder came to be merged with the revived role of sacrificial priest. Once we recognize that coordinating ministry and leading worship are different abilities, we can disentangle the roles and use a council of elders as it was used originally.

This organizational model recognizes the wisdom and leadership skills of those who live and work in the community, those who have emerged as its own natural leaders. It also ensures that decisions made and directions chosen come from the lived experience of the community, not from "on high."

The council of elders was organized so that three of its members, one-third, would be relieved each year and enabled to return to their primary ministries. There is no problem with status, and administrative and directive duties remain secondary to service beyond the community.

In some places, this can be done with the full cooperation of a whole parish. For many people, however, church is a smaller base community, either within or independent of a structured parish. The beauty of this process is that it can be done by a group of any size—to shift gears from the endless *talk about* ministry to *action*—and depends only on the consent of the members.

Discussion Questions

1. Name as many ministry needs of your area as you can. Look beyond the physical needs of parish buildings.

2. How did you feel when you were doing step 4, gift discernment, with your discussion group or with a friend?

3. Which community members remind you of elders: they keep others aware of needs, coordinate helpers, keep you centered?

4. Do you think going through the whole process of shared ministry might help *your* community "shift gears from talk to action"? Would it be a good idea?

7

Hard Choices: Inching toward a Postclerical Age

Of course, many local communities within the Roman Catholic Church have changed radically for the better. But on the whole the originally medieval system remains in operation and keeps on distinguishing the very being of each male cleric from the lesser being of each of the faithful, and all that on the basis of an antiquated and highly questionable sacramental theology. (Werner G. Jeanrond, in POBAL: the Laity in Ireland, Sean MacReamoinn, ed. [Dublin: Columba Press, 1986], p. 31)

In years past, one's connection with church was through the person of the pastor or other local clergymen. But once people have an experience of church community today, *that* becomes the center and connecting point for them.

Operating on the vertical image of church, all decisions and most ideas originated in the rectory. One always needed to ask permission to step out of ranks or deviate from the program. After an experience of something like shared ministry, the source of energy for action is also in the community. Responsibility rests there, and from it comes the confidence to make decisions.

Our working model of church is moving ahead, and we are part of that movement. As one of my friends used to say, there is no putting the toothpaste back in the tube. It would be hard for some of us to ever go back to the old-style passive/ authoritarian model. And yet, unsure or unable to let go of some of the old baggage, we are inching our way along, laboring under the weight of it. Sometimes we must look like a band of westward-bound settlers in the covered-wagon days, carrying along a whole set of heavy baroque furniture.

The point of this chapter—and, ultimately, this book—is to reconsider our journey to this point, scout the terrain ahead, and decide whether to keep the furniture and settle on the leeward side of the mountains, or to lighten the load and make it all the way to the coast. It is time to ask the hard questions, to begin to make the hard choices.

Are We Serious about Our Commitment to Be Church?

Each community comes to a point where this question will determine all the rest. If church is *one* person's responsibility—if someone is "pastor" and all the others are "sheep"— then we can be passive, "attend" services done by others, and those services will continue. But church is *our* responsibility— even if we delegate one of our number to be a coordinator— continuity will *depend* on our personal investment of time and energy.

The 1971 film *McCabe and Mrs. Miller* is a caricature of this kind of contrast. The setting is "Presbyterian Church, Oregon," a turn-of-the-century town inhabited by gold prospectors, prostitutes, and others willing to trade the mores and morals of civilization for the lure of a quick fortune. The pride and namesake of the town was the structure with the steeple, built with their profits—*not* to change or influence the prevailing lifestyle, not even for their own attendance—but because every town should have one.

Communities that need to "have a church" and even attend one, but choose to maintain a minimal level of participation, will probably not encounter the questions that this chapter poses. Those who choose to graduate from passive inactivity and accept responsibility for their Christian life and growth will run head-on into all the questions that follow. The degree of their commitment will determine the outcome; without prayer, reiterated awareness of the gospel message and of the Spirit-among-us, and great personal investment on the part of the whole local church family, the journey toward new church, living church, will flounder.

How Can a Community Choose a Like-minded Coordinator?

The diocesan clergy personnel board held a meeting at a local parish to sound out the parish's expectations before assigning a new pastor. (The term "pastor" is already loaded with implications for his relationship with them.) The only view articulated at the meeting was that of an active subcommunity of the parish: they wanted someone who would work *with them* in their ministries and *help them* celebrate Jesus' presence liturgically.

After a passage of time, a priest was sent. His concept of church is fifty years behind that of the base community. What are their choices?

Who among the Community Should Preach?

Sermons are a painful subject. Ideally, this part of the weekly gathering should focus the light of the scripture readings on the experiences and responsibilities peculiar to those persons in that neighborhood. Who has the gift of making connections between the gospel and *their* day-to-day living?

What if the person appointed to do this does not have the gift for it? What if he does not know the membership, or has no ideas about how scripture intersects with *their* life? What if he has nothing to say? What if all he can do is rewarm comments written thirty years ago, or deliver a mail-order reflection, prewritten for "any" audience? What can the community do to fill this void, or are the members expected to just "make do" for the six-year term?

Can a Community Determine Its Own Ministries?

In the late 1970s, when our area was in the depths of a recession, and many of us were out of work and hard pressed to keep ahead of the bill collector, construction was undertaken on a new worship facility. The decision was the pastor's alone. To his way of thinking, parish funds and energies should all be directed to the physical plant.

Old-school parishioners dutifully made their financial pledges; but service-minded types decried the extravagance of a new building and, what is worse, the many stained-glass windows, hand-carved altar, and air-conditioning in an area where few could afford it at home. What voice do parishioners have in determining the use of their resources for ministry?

What about Parish Councils?

The establishment of parish councils, in many areas, has conceded only the right to talk. Current practice puts councils on a par with the tooth fairy. The child goes through the ritual of putting the baby tooth under the pillow, and in the morning there is a coin in its place. The child does not know that a parent—not the tooth fairy—made the exchange during the night. Similarly, parish council members go through their rituals of parliamentary procedure and, at the next meeting, the decision appears before them. But it was done late at night by the pastor alone, or by the bishop or some diocesan board, not by them.

A friend recently told me of a California parish where the pastor refused to permit the council to discuss any outreach ministries until his new construction project was completed. The traditional Thanksgiving and Christmas collections of food for the poor were postponed indefinitely. The council members decided it was useless to meet under those circumstances, so they disbanded. What else could they have done?

Down to the Basics: The Right and Responsibility to Create Church

We have come a long way in the last twenty years. But we are just now approaching some of the questions at the heart of the matter. What are the rights and responsibilities of the baptized Christian? What is still reserved to a sacral caste, and why?

The first letter to the Corinthians reflects an early awareness that the Spirit empowered *all* members with gifts for the building up of the community. Baptism—membership in the Christian community—carried with it a call to use one's gifts for others, to incarnate Jesus in the world. There was a wide range of gifts recognized and used in many ministries: first the apostles, then prophets and teachers, then miracle-workers and healers and those with the ability to help others.

Those who work closely enough with one another in local communities recognize that the same Spirit and, therefore, those same gifts are still present and operative today.

Who, then, in our local churches are the apostles?

The best definition I have heard of apostle is a disciple who has come of age and is able to be sent forth. The apostle has a hunger that drives her or him out of self and into a personal encounter with the Lord Jesus, enabling that person to help others direct *their* hunger and celebrate *their* new life. Who really does have that drive, that sense of intimacy with Jesus and with others?

Then come the prophets, often countercultural, who preach the word in its radical clarity. They dare to challenge the institution to let go of human ways and center on the Lord's way, and they suffer for it. Who are our prophets?

The gift and ministry of teaching comes next, and there are many who "sew tents" and raise families, yet find time to go to night school so that they have more to share with others. They are co-seekers with their students of the riches of the gospel.

There have always been coordinators and administrators, too. In the early days, a council of presbyters/elders was elected from within the local community to coordinate, facilitate, and prioritize goals.

It takes many gifts, including many different leadership gifts working side by side, members of the community first, and delegated to serve within that community and beyond, to make church a living reality. It is a work of the whole community, and is exercised by each one according to each one's God-given talents.

Untangling Leadership from a Clerical State

What does all this say to our current two-tiered institution? Where do "clerics" fit into a committed community: those chosen by lot (its original meaning), or "clerks," the bookkeepers and administrators? How do we justify the continued use of "lay person" with its connotation of ignorant, unskilled, and uninvolved?

A congregation that is content to remain passive and let someone else provide convenient services will not experience this conflict. But when that congregation "grows up" to become a vibrant community of committed, intelligent, adult Christians, what are they to do with the man who walks in and assumes the right to make all decisions and control all liturgical celebrations? What is his place among them: does "clergy" describe a function—that should presume a gift—or an elevated state of being?

Do the clerics own *all* the gifts of leadership in the local churches? Many are good administrators, but some are not. Only some have the gift to teach. A few have the drive of apostles but they are found more often on the lecture circuit than settled in neighborhoods. And prophecy is still barely tolerated. (The *Chicago Tribune* noted that the young cleric who repeatedly raised the issue of neighborhood street gangs "had not been invited" to the cardinal's private meeting on the subject.) How, then, can priests be considered to "have a call" to do something for which they do not have the gifts?

Ordination, as we presently use it, calls gifts to service *only when they are present*. The rest of the time, we confer "office" —we commission someone to act on behalf of the community—whether the appropriate gifts are present or not, and we *fail* to commission many who *do* have those gifts. Some communities have had no real "celebrant" for years. Some have apostles, prophets, teachers, and healers—actually *using* their gifts in ministry—but the only one formally commissioned is the administrator, and that individual often will neither work *with* the community nor *in* it.

The Old Ecclesiastical Monarchy

Our working ecclesiology up to the present was built on a monarchical model. Seminary-trained individuals were raised to ecclesiastical "royalty"; clergy represented the authority of God and king. It was all so mysterious and beyond us: Latin names for all the changes that were supposed to happen in a man when a certain other man laid hands on him. *Res et sacramentum*, the sacred seal, the indelible sign, "mark on the soul," *the power*—for life.

A system based on so narrow a vision of ministry and community empowerment has become not only unresponsive to change and growth, but antagonistic to it.

Until recently it was assumed that the man who was publicly commissioned/ordained as leader had all the gifts to lead, or received them with the office. Communities today are finding gaps in that assumption:

1. The man in question may not have any qualities of leadership at all.
2. Among the personalities who comprise a particular community, he may not stand out as their leader.
3. One who has the gifts to lead a group at a particular time will not necessarily have what it takes to lead them for all times and through all other events.

The question facing our communities is not whether we need someone to preach, to counsel, to coordinate. All these are needed, and more. The question is whether we can continue to give any *one* person the sole responsibility for all those ministries—for life—without asking whether that person is the best one for that ministry, at that time, in that community.

A New Ecclesiology

The designation of a sacral class as owner and controller of ministry is diametrically opposed to the correlative ideas of the *universal* call to ministry and universal participation in the *one* priesthood of Jesus—ideas that originally funded Christianity.

The birth of living church requires a "new" ecclesiology based on the conversion commitment of baptism, the universal call to ministry, and grateful recognition of the gifts of in-house leadership as they appear in the life of a community. It will not do to try to lengthen the umbilical cord by creating new ways to "help Father," or giving others the rank of "little father." It is possible to have order—fidelity to the gospel and networking —without the whole power/exclusivity package that a clerical state represents.

The apostles, prophets, teachers, and healers are all there now in our local communities. Some have been commissioned/ ordained in public ceremony and some are commissioned/ ordained by the recognition and respect of the community.

Communities that use a process like shared ministry already have incorporated rites of commissioning into the recurring rhythm of life.

Our era right now is called to make a major adjustment in our working ecclesiology, to recognize the shift of the center of gravity from the few to the many, to widen our scope of ministry and our use of commissioning/ordination. We are faced with the choice of whether or not to put down the heavy monarchical trappings of the past in order to move into a simpler, more challenging life in a new land. There are base communities worldwide already doing this, wondering when the rest will catch up.

Discussion Questions

1. Who is a prophet in your community—who takes the risk of speaking out when the community gets away from gospel/scriptural priorities?

2. Name any contemporary prophets, in the public eye or in a small community, who have influenced you personally.

3. In your small community, who has the ability to make peace, to explain things, to get you to take action? What other gifts do you see in action? How might the community recognize those gifts?

4. What would you think about commissioning individuals to use particular gifts, including leadership at worship, for a limited period of time instead of for life?

5. If we all started using our gifts more actively, what term(s) could we use to designate our relationship to each other instead of "clergy" and "laity," "cleric" and "lay person"?

8

Responsibility or Co-dependence?

When you believe that you are not a legitimate human being in and of yourself, and that your legitimacy hinges on outside validation and approval, you live in constant fear. You are uneasy about trusting your own perceptions and feelings, because there is always the chance that they will differ from those of the people who give you legitimacy. When they do in fact differ, it feels like psychological annihilation. (Anne Wilson Schaef, When Society Becomes an Addict *[San Francisco: Harper & Row, 1987], p. 93)*

There is an understanding emerging from the study of family systems that provides marvelous insights for our current struggle as emerging church. This is the whole concept of co-dependence. It is the latest in a long line of studies on relationships between home life and behavior patterns.

The evolution of this concept started with the formation of Alcoholics Anonymous and the support group for spouses of alcoholics, Al-Anon. Therapists who worked with these people discovered that the personalities of those who *live with* alcoholics have a number of traits in common.

As treatment widened to include whole families, counselors documented a set of behavior patterns common to all families in which one member was addicted to alcohol. Since then, the same behavior patterns have been found to be typical of all types of dysfunctional families.

A dysfunctional family is one where one person is addicted to alcohol, prescription drugs, street drugs, food, or any other substance, has a compulsive personality with periods of workaholism, abuse (verbal, psychological, or sexual), or emotional withdrawal. Any family where the members cannot connect with each other or bond with each other on a feeling level is *not working* as a family and, hence, is called dysfunctional. Any high-stress, emotionally repressed situation can be included under the heading "dysfunctional."

This is the pattern. The spouse is usually the enabler, covering for the alcoholic and working overtime to convince the neighbors that "we're all fine." One of the children, frequently the eldest, fills the role of the family hero: the picture of success in school but inwardly insecure, feeling responsible to make the parent happy so he or she will not withdraw, will not have to drink.

Another child is the scapegoat, always in trouble, someone the family can blame for their pain. The lost child is the quiet one; she or he provides relief—no problems—but develops little sense of self or emotion. And then there is the mascot, who uses humor and other means to distract attention from the problem.

All these people learn to do whatever the current state of crisis needs or allows them to do; they take their cues from the mood of the alcoholic.

The most recent studies, books that are appearing this year, point to a deeper problem that we carry with us from dysfunctional families. This is the problem *behind* the addictions and behind a host of unhealthy relationships, what "drives a person to drink" and to give and take abuse—a pattern called codependence.

Persons without Centers

Rich Anderson of Cambridge, Minnesota, has given the best definition I have heard of co-dependence: it is a patterned way of relating to others with low self-esteem at one's core. We learn the pattern while living in a dysfunctional system, from someone who already practices it.

The spouse of a chemically dependent person, the prime enabler whose every choice and action revolves around that troubled person, teaches the children how to make *their* lives revolve around that other, too. It works like this. We learn to focus all our attention and energies on the addictive/compulsive person, to smooth out the wrinkles in his or her life so that he or she does not have to drink (or take pills, or withdraw)— we hope—and to compensate for the problems that occur when he or she does.

We learn to deny our own ideas and feelings. There is no room for "I think that . . ." or "I'm feeling . . ." or "I'd like. . . ." We are told what to think and what we can feel. We are told that Dad just works too hard and needs to relax. Or Mom does not feel well, she is tired, she needs quiet so she can rest. We are told we do not feel anger—that is not nice. We do not really hate—that is not Christian.

If I think Dad is an alcoholic, I must be disloyal. If all my ideas are wrong and all my feelings cannot really be my feelings, then I must be crazy. So I stop thinking and feeling, and I do what I am told.

A co-dependent person has little or no self-worth. It would be misleading to say that the target person has worth and the co-dependent does not, because with co-dependence comes a self-righteousness that the other person is hurting himself (herself) and the family, and that he (she) should change. But in terms of the proportion of emotional energy spent, we would have to say most is spent on the other person, even at the cost of one's own health or growth or development.

Co-dependence is like cutting out one's center and handing it to someone else. There is a hole where the person ought to be, and that person's own center of perception and decision-making and activity is now located in someone else. In a dysfunctional family, there are holes where *several* persons ought to be. No one acts autonomously. All only *react* to the needs and the moods of the addicted or compulsive person.

The Warped Cart

The family system becomes like a four-wheel cart with one odd-sized wheel. The whole cart is tilted. All the other wheels have to move on a slant to accommodate the odd wheel. That slantedness is co-dependence.

A normal wheel that moves around its own center has a sense of straight and a sense of direction. The wheels on the warped cart have no centers. Their centers—their sense of rightness and sense of direction—have been cut out and placed in the odd wheel. Having one's center and sense of direction in someone else is co-dependence.

In the Midwest, because of the heavy snow we can expect in the winter, cars with front-wheel drive have become popular. The motor moves the two front wheels and they can pull the car forward, out of the snow-packed driveway. Even better are the four-wheel drive vehicles because each of the four wheels is powered by the engine and helps to move the car. A co-dependent system is like a car with one-wheel drive. Only the right front wheel is powered by the motor, so the car is dragged along, straining and leaning to one side as it goes.

Co-dependence: A Sickness

In dysfunctional systems, the co-dependent members are slavishly attached to their target person who is chemically dependent or compulsive or emotionally absent. They may or may not be aware that *that* person is sick. What they do not see is that *their own behavior* is a sickness.

Even if the addicted or compulsive person changes, or dies, or goes away, *they* will still be co-dependent unless they get help.

We learn co-dependence at home and carry it into all our other relationships because we have learned to give our center to someone else. We have no consciousness of what we as individuals think or feel or need.

Wanting Change but Fighting Change

Co-dependent people want their troubled person to change, to give up the habit that is destroying the life of the family. On the other hand, they are afraid of change, in general, for fear they will lose the little they have. They have no secure center, so they cling rigidly to a pattern of behavior that actually perpetuates the problem.

A typical pattern would be to offer excuses why the family will not be attending the party or has to leave early—Mom is tired, or Dad does not feel well. To go ahead with family plans without that parent when he or she is unable to participate would be "disloyal," unthinkable. The family takes its cues from the dependent person, follows a "safe" and predictable pattern, and keeps the person with the problem insulated from any of its ill effects. We avoid ugly scenes, we avoid moments of crisis, but we postpone indefinitely the person's need to change.

The Only Way Out

Most co-dependents think that the only way out of their predicament is for the addicted/compulsive person to change. To that end, they may even lecture, sabotage, or bargain with that person to *make* him or her change. But it does not work. It never works, and for two reasons:

1. As long as someone *else* is willing to take responsibility, the addicted/compulsive person *never* has to.
2. The more one's attention becomes riveted on someone else, the more deeply co-dependent one is.

There is only *one* way out of co-dependence, only one hope for oneself and for the system, and that is to *change oneself*: to develop a strong sense of self—ideas, feelings, talents, goals; to find a new pattern of behavior, a new role model; to get support—people who have made or are making the change, who will affirm that growing sense of autonomy, who will give encouragement when needed.

The Co-dependent Church

We learn co-dependence in a dysfunctional system, and many families fit the pattern. But the home we grew up in and the home we are making for our children now are not the only families we belong to. Other institutions in our society have been identified as teaching and encouraging co-dependence.

One morning this summer I was having breakfast with two women from two other parishes, each involved in the catechumenate—RCIA—in their respective parishes. They were describing to each other the frustration they were experiencing.

There are four priests involved in our program, one said, two from our parish and two from the parish down the road. Each priest comes to only one meeting, gives a dry, theoretical lecture, and leaves. They will not make it personal, and they will not let us do it either. They will not allow open discussion or sharing stories—that takes too much time. I said I could moderate a discussion period if they want to leave early, but they said no, there could be no meetings without them.

I have been telling myself they're too busy, she continued, but they are *not* too busy. Almost nothing happens in our parish. They never visit the people. They do not even put in a forty-hour week. Here I *do* work a regular job, plus all the scheduling, calling, setting up for this. Still, I cannot get their permission to do something that will let the people get some sense of community. I am so tired, but no matter what I do, I cannot seem to get them to change.

A System That Cuts the Centers Out

The problem is not just with the clergy; it is the whole system that cuts the centers out of most persons and puts the centers in a few. The associate pastor in this woman's parish was himself pointing further up the clerical line and saying that *he* could not do anything because "disagreements aren't allowed" among the older priests. His center was in someone else, too.

The other woman at breakfast said that the clergy at her parish know the initiation process with their heads, but will not let themselves participate on a personal level—share experiences, share feelings; there was no personal presence when they gather. She, too, has tried all sorts of approaches to help them see the lack. I am so tired, she said, but I do not know how to get them to change.

I was listening to all this, feeling with them the deep frustration that I too have experienced in so many similar situations. They are eager to share but unable to act. Their right to act has been vested in someone else. The authenticity of their views depends on concurrence with someone else's views.

Then I realized we are caught in another co-dependent system. We call it church—we call it family—and like so many other families, the pattern of behavior is undeniably dysfunctional: co-dependent.

"They" or "We"

The most telling sign of co-dependence is that church is still *"they"* to most members. The news services published opinion polls in anticipation of the pope's visit in September 1987. Two-thirds of American Catholics stated openly that they disagreed with John Paul on birth control. Yet they will tell you that "the church" holds that birth control is wrong. How many Catholics must agree before it can be said that the church accepts it, or at least that the church has more than one opinion? Or is the church always someone else?

For many, parish life is like life with an alcoholic: slavish dependence on another, all the while hoping he will change. Many will admit they tell the pastor only what he wants to hear. They *see* a need, but will not *do* anything about it until he sees it too. They have talents to share, but settle for serving cake and coffee. They are becoming burned out for want of some honest communication, some people-touching-people community, but will ignore or deny those legitimate needs until someone tells them it is all right to have them.

Many of us are or have been caught in the same system of co-dependence. We see others in need, we know some simple and direct actions that ought to be taken to care for them, yet we do not allow ourselves to see what we see, or know what we know, until someone else blesses our opinion. That is co-dependence.

What if I want to start a "Rainbow" ministry for children of divorced parents? There are so many children who need to sort it all out, who need help so that they will not blame themselves. The person in charge says no, you cannot—we have too many programs already. So I give it up—I must have been wrong. That's co-dependence.

What if I want to start ministry to the Spanish-speaking, but spend years trying to convince the pastor to give me permission. That is co-dependence.

If I make it my career to try to make the other person change, that is co-dependence. To focus on someone else and spend all my energies on that person is to continue to behave according to the rules of a sick system, a system that does not work. We end up perpetuating the very problem we are trying so desperately to end. The only way out of a co-dependent system is to change oneself.

Why Do We Need to Change?

The worst part of co-dependence is that it takes the place of *discipleship*. Look at the early church. All members were keenly aware that the Spirit who gave direction and energy to Jesus' ministry would direct them as they used their own gifts and talents to care for the needy around them. They knew that if others were to be touched by God's loving care, *they* would have to do the touching; if others were to be embraced and reconciled and healed, *they* would have to do the hugging. They knew that if the hungry were to be fed with food and with hope, *they* would have to do the feeding.

There was networking, bouncing ideas back and forth, room for healthy disagreement. Persons could be themselves and serve. Discipleship meant ministry, and ministry was everyone's call, everyone's responsibility.

Do you see what we do to discipleship today when we say that only a few have the right to see needs? Only a few have the right to initiate service? Only a few have the right to say in what limited way others may own or use their talents?

This is worse than a four-wheel cart with one-wheel drive: in many Christian assemblies, only one wheel in two-hundred or one in a thousand is connected to an engine.

This is a gross distortion of the meaning of Christian discipleship and, therefore, of the meaning of church. Instead of a family that promotes the wholeness and holiness of all God's children—that tells the woman bent over for eighteen years that she may now stand up straight; instead of a church that embodies Jesus' care and the good news of his message— we have a crippled system that teaches and encourages co-dependence.

Why should we change ourselves? Because discipleship is not devotion to protocol; that was getting in the way back in Jesus' day. The discipleship he taught is a matter of simple service—caring for the real needs of real persons—and sharing the good news as *good news.*

Why should we change ourselves? Because discipleship demands a *whole* person, not one with a hole in the middle. It requires people both aware of the needs around them and able to respond to those needs. It takes both courage and initiative to bring God's love to others.

Why do we need to change? Families, institutions, relationships can be destroyed by co-dependence. Many divorces, many struggling marriages, give evidence of this. The control-compliance pattern only brings out the worst in each of the partners. Couples can struggle along, doing the only thing they know how to do, doing what their parents did, until they get so tired and so hurt that they walk away from the marriage.

If they get help, they can introduce the only hope there is for this kind of change: learning new patterns of interaction. Still, for couples who finally do get help and give their marriage new life, it is hard to look back and know they wasted so much time.

In a world where patterns of superiority and protectionism breed such hostility that we live on the brink of destruction, in a world where insecurity and fear destroy families with addiction and abuse, we cannot afford to spend church time just playing games. We are called to give hope, but we are wasting so much time, and we do not have time to waste.

Does that mean that in this moment of crisis we should try all the more to change the system?

If we are still telling ourselves that the problem is the institution, we are fooling ourselves. The problem is that *we* have been willing to give our sense of self and sense of direction to someone else and leave a hole in ourselves. The problem is that we have made our own responsibilities contingent on someone else's, and therefore we have never had to act. The problem is our own co-dependence. The only way to change that system is to *change ourselves*.

How Can We Change?

We need to do three things to break this cycle of co-dependence.

Develop a strong sense of self—take seriously Jesus' message about each one's worth. Each one *is* important; each one *can* make a difference. We need to get in touch with our ideas for ministries, our own goals, and what we personally need from church in the way of support.

It is necessary to find our edges: to know what I think and what I feel, and be able to compare them with the thoughts and feelings of others, to know that my own thoughts and experiences have their own right to exist.

A New System/Pattern of Behavior

We need to be reminded often that there is another way of thinking and acting. Jesus repeatedly affirmed the worth of *each* person, invited each one to contribute their *own* gifts to the building of the kingdom. That message is the antidote to our present co-dependent system: we need megadoses of gospel. The early church used only enough structure to support the community: we need to nourish and support ourselves with the Acts of the Apostles.

Scripture helps us keep the center in the center. The reading is simple, short, and makes the point that the kingdom should be our first priority—ahead of denomination, ahead of certification, ahead of programs. And we build the kingdom by letting God's good-news-in-real-life speak louder than our own philosophical formulations, by letting our simple service to others be more important than getting others into our programs.

Support

To live with a healthy sense of self and a sound pattern of interaction we need to surround ourselves with others who share the vision and values of the gospel and Acts. Those persons become our support system—keep us centered, keep us from losing heart.

Scott Peck, in his book *The Different Drum: Community Building and Peace* (New York: Simon and Schuster, 1987), counts most church communities as "pseudo communities." In contrast, *real* communities are open systems, where members are committed, open, vulnerable, loving, free, equal, and inclusive (p. 165). Real community is consistent with Jesus' instruction that his disciples not lord it over one another, and that mutual love be their hallmark. Real community enables *each one* of its members to come to wholeness, to make their unique contribution to the ongoing work of God, to live in loving communion with humankind and with God. Its work is both wholeness and holiness, both creation and salvation.

Getting support means building base communities. Church happens when two or three are gathered in Jesus' name. It is time to gather—with like-minded people—to keep each other focused on the gospel, affirmed in our talents, encouraged to serve. We need to serve together, pray together, celebrate and eat together.

No More Games

It is time to stand together and say, "No more games." The decision to break the cycle of co-dependence and move ahead into health and holiness means to resolve not to play any more games—not to do programs for their own sake, or just because we have done them before—they take the place of our real goals.

It is typical of dysfunctional families to put great stock in the externals of family but miss out on personal presence. There is a great show—see how everyone gets along!—but no real sharing on a deeper level. We do that all too often in our churches.

We have become content to process children—adults, too—through programs without any real sharing of the experiences that tie our lives together. People collect sacraments like girl scouts collect badges, but what is happening inside?

We are still waiting for someone else to change so our true Christian life can begin, still waiting to use our gifts in ministry until someone tells us we may. We have all the best intentions, and would be doing more now, but we are waiting for *him*, or *them*, to change.

This pattern absolves *us* of any responsibility. We say that *they* must take the initiative; but our compliance ensures they never will. We allow ourselves to think that we need only follow—only react. And given the dysfunctional character of this family, that keeps us free from all but very predictable and, therefore, *safe* kinds of activity.

In terms of our role in church, we have permitted ourselves to take satisfaction from bearing with the injustice of the system, instead of taking the risk to work for the kingdom. We say we give our centers to Jesus, but this pattern is not his gospel. We waste our talents, and sell out the one thing that could offer hope: our own healthy discipleship.

Becoming a Healthy Church Family

To get started, Christians have to promise each other that we will keep the center in the center—share the news of God's love and work to build kingdom—and that we will not process people anymore, that any time we are involved in any interaction *as church*, we will make it an opportunity for building of real community and the building of God's kingdom. We have to involve our youth and our newcomers in our own lives and in experiences of real ministries, whether or not they manage to get all the word games in the workbook completed.

We have to make it a habit to reflect together after those experiences, to pray together and to share food together, for that is the healthful pattern we were originally given.

Church needs to be a place where each one is respected, each one is heard, each one's needs are ministered to, each one's talents are affirmed and used, where love and energies spill over to help all those around them.

Christians today can make a choice for healthy living. The alternative is to be like the wife (or husband) of an alcoholic who watches the children drift away in disgust and pain while she (he) wrings her (his) hands and says, "But what can I do?" Like her (him), we can stay as addicted to the addict as he (she) is to drink, and never own ourselves, and never have to change. The trouble with that option is that if we are addicted to a system for security, we will not recognize the Spirit when the Spirit calls.

The Question of Protest

Does all this mean we have no right to try to change unjust institutions by protest or other means? That depends on one's act of protest. Is it saying, "please give us a piece of what is rightfully *yours*," or "we are claiming what is rightfully *ours*"? The first is the plea of the co-dependent; the second the assertion of one who is sure.

The most effective protests in the past have been those in which people claimed the rights they knew were due them: blacks sat in the front of the bus, registered for school, and registered to vote; Gandhi and the people of India made salt.

Most of what we are called to do does not happen in the sanctuary, but in homes and in the marketplace. Most does not require permission, by anyone's measure. The rest—it is time to look at that, too.

Are we ready to be sisters and brothers? Then we need to stop playing house, and start being a healthy family.

Are we ready to be disciples? Then we need to stop playing royalty, and start building the kingdom.

Discussion Questions

1. "They are eager to share but unable to act. Their right to act has been vested in someone else. The authenticity of their views depends on the concurrence of someone else's views." Does this match with your experience? Explain.

2. "Discipleship is not devotion to protocol. . . . It requires a *whole* person, not one with a hole in the middle." What does that say to you? to your small community?

3. Discuss: "the only way to change the system is to change *ourselves*."

4. "It is time to stand together and say 'no more games.' " Where are you standing?

9

Cutting the Cord: Restoring Eucharist to the Community

After all, if is far easier to think of intimacy with God solely in terms of our relating to HIM. Redemptive intimacy becomes so much more difficult for us if God has been so indiscreet as to have identified himself with all of humankind. It would mean that the route to divine intimacy runs through the whole human race! (*Dick Westley*, Redemptive Intimacy [*Mystic, Conn.: Twenty-Third Publications, 1981*])

From the mid-1960s until late 1971, in spite of the turmoil over authority and moral issues, my experience of church as a worshiping community was excellent. It was always possible to find both presiders and participants in college environments whose liturgies were joyous and open and warm, true celebrations of their wider involvement in service and commitment to each other.

All that changed when my husband and I returned to mainstream parish life in the 1970s. The experiences of that period again challenged my concept of church and were the occasion of applying newer concepts of church to a widening scope of situations.

I discovered that there was a significant number of pastors whose relationship with the faithful was based on the "divine right of kings." The parish was their job; their friends were elsewhere. Lacking that sense of community, liturgies were dead and dry, ritualistic, anonymous. Decisions were typically arbitrary, with consideration of the clock, the bottom line, and hierarchical politics ahead of and instead of the real needs of people.

Even when we finally found a worshiping community that managed to establish and maintain a spirit of mutual support and service—real Christian community—we found that its expression of Jesus' presence and its commitment in Sunday worship could be sabotaged by a presider who had no sense whatever of that community or of its experience of church.

I had grown up with the certainty that it was the power of the ordained presider that "made Jesus present" at our eucharist. But I found myself in a situation where the pompousness, the coldness, the pride of office of the ordained presider stood in contrast to the sense of welcome and healing I experienced in the people. Jesus said, "By their fruits you shall know them." What I saw, Sunday after Sunday, was the antithesis of what I had learned: the man in the center was going through a ritual, but the community of people standing in a circle around the altar, speaking to each other with their eyes and hearts—*they* were celebrating eucharist.

"Where two or three are gathered in my name, there I am in their midst." Had there always been an implicit proviso that one of the three be ordained? If I had not encountered the particular set of experiences I did, I probably would never have questioned it. But as many times as I was forced to ask "Can this really be church?" or "Does it have to be this way?" the answer was more basic. And the simpler the picture of church became, the more closely it began to resemble the experience of the earliest followers of Jesus.

Given the choice between "keeping kosher" and breaking bread with a believing, ministering community, I will choose community every time. What finally convinced me to write this book is the discovery of how many other people are making the same choice.

The Current "Crisis"

In some areas the decline of the number of celibate, seminary-trained men has left some communities without the celebration of eucharist for weeks at a time. Articles have begun to appear on how to fill the void. Some communities have implemented prayer services of various sorts. Others have a visiting cleric consecrate quantities of bread at a monthly eucharist. Then each week, the community gathers for a service that resembles eucharist but without the eucharistic prayer, without entering into the whole dynamic of eucharist. There is no bringing of this week's loaf—all of us as we have been kneaded together by this week's experiences and ministries—into the ever-present event of Jesus' passover, no symbolic crossing over with him from death to new life.

What we have instead resembles the school children's token reenactment of Thanksgiving—a story and a piece of corn-bread is no family feast!

If we are starting with the assumption that eucharist must decline, if we are asking who *else* might be processed to do it or what *else* we might pray instead, we are asking the wrong questions. We are trying to get to the next square on the sidewalk instead of looking to see if we might be on the wrong street.

Where Does Eucharist Come from?

First, to understand the ancient roots of eucharist, we need to look at two Jewish celebrations that were part of Jesus' life: passover and the Sabbath supper. Passover is celebrated annually in the spring to commemorate the passage from slavery to freedom that the Lord God had wrought. It is a thanksgiving: for spring rains, for plentiful food, for family, for heritage, for deliverance from the pharoah and all oppression, even thanksgiving for help and guidance yet to be received. The feast is as rich in traditional foods as it is in traditional prayers, family-centered and joyous.

Passover is also a joining with every past generation in experiencing God's deliverance: all, together, have been led to freedom.

The Friday-night Sabbath supper is a weekly celebration of Jewish heritage. Each head of household would gather his family and lead them in the prayers of thanksgiving. A rabbi would sup with his students to reflect with them on the traditions of their people and to engage them in discussion. This would have been the weekly custom for the rabbi from Nazareth too, and his band of fishermen-students.

These feasts that formed the rhythm of Jesus' life were the context from which eucharist developed. Jesus added further nuances to celebrations that were already a regular part of his and his friends' lives. Celebration of the ancient journey was a celebration of the journey of life, and the journey of life was seen as a journey to God. But the ancient roots of eucharist tell only half the story. Eucharist has a source in the present as well.

Jesus' *life* was a passover: an overall attitude of thanksgiving to God, a passage through obstacles and pain to life. His death and resurrection were the last part of the passage. Incorporation into Jesus—I mean the *conscious* joining of one's life to his—means passing through many deaths to life and in the same spirit/Spirit of thanksgiving. Christian life is a continuing passover.

Now those aspects of life that are most important, that are central to our sense of what our life is really about, are given special attention regularly to refocus their meaning and to reaffirm their position of priority. That is why Sabbath suppers (then as now) celebrated throughout the year all that is good in Jewish heritage, and why the early followers of Jesus sought each other out regularly—to reaffirm all that bonded them to Jesus and each other, and to continue together on their passover.

Consider the place of lovemaking in a good, loving marriage. It is an intense moment in which the whole of married life is summed up—the excitement of new beginnings and the tedium of daily routine, the wounds both given and received, and the salve of forgiveness, the letting go of pettiness and holding on to each other. Lovemaking is a moment in which mutual commitment to one another is reaffirmed and again given central priority. For those who understand its place in the rhythm of a committed relationship, it becomes a means to better understand eucharist.

The eucharist is a gathering of Jesus' friends, in his memory and with him present, to celebrate the passover meal of our deliverance. We celebrate freedom from bondage and the new life of the Spirit that fills us, makes us one. The eucharist is to the Christian community what lovemaking is to a marriage: a summing up of the pain and the growth, the hurt and the forgiving, the love and the life that continually renew that relationship.

We the church are a community with Jesus, alive and with us. We are intimates, committed to a basic attitude of thanksgiving to God and a vision of passage to fuller life. Eucharist is our most intense moment of reunion and re-creation, all of us together with Jesus. It is a moment oft repeated as part of the rhythm of life, a moment of refocusing and recommitment. It is literally "lovemaking."

Eucharist flows from the nature of Christian community life, a part of the rhythm of life for those who have answered Jesus' call to follow and have found themselves—not alone with him— but in a "circle of twelve," trying to make the journey together and with him.

So eucharist comes from two sources—one in the past and one in the present. It developed from Jewish traditions, the annual celebration of deliverance and the weekly recentering of their heritage. At the same time but in a different respect, eucharist arises from the rhythm of Spirit-filled Christian community life.

Why Did It Change?

As chapter 1 describes, the early followers of Jesus gathered in small household communities. They all knew each other well, and together lived a vision of life that was different from that of any of the main religious movements of the time. They were in the minority, countercultural. They gathered quietly, sometimes at risk; their gatherings were small and intimate, simple and spontaneous.

When Christianity became mandatory throughout the Roman empire, new members were joining as whole towns, with no sense of the spirit or mission of Jesus, merely a sense of survival. Jesus was pictured as another emperor, robed in glory and ruling in majesty. Jesus-our-brother was forgotten, along with any sense of family among Christians. Congregations grew larger, more anonymous, more stratified, the gatherings more like performances.

Christians of the Middle Ages saw church differently from Christians of the first century. They did not see *themselves* as church—"church" was the central body of authority, to which they were connected by way of a clerical "cord." Local congregations were dependent on the "central office" to send in leadership, someone who could answer questions, protect orthodoxy, "perform" sacraments. That mentality survived unchanged, unchallenged, until Vatican II.

I remember growing up with a sense of security that as long as somebody was "up there" at the helm, I was safe, in good hands, if somewhat passive. God was in his heaven (the pope in Rome, the bishop in his chancery, the pastor in his rectory . . .) and all was right with the world. It became so comfortable that a large number of us in the Western world were passive Christians. We were comfortable with a core of "professional" Christians in a mass of "laypersons," and comfort tends to stifle occasional doubts about passivity.

We are just now waking up to see that the price of that kind of comfort, in many areas already, is eucharist. The womb, once so comfortable, is now cramped and confining. And the articles on substitutes for eucharist are only suggesting ways we can devise to lengthen the umbilical cord.

I chose "cord" because it should be a means of getting nourishment from a parent to a child whose lack of development makes feeding himself impossible. The clerical cord evolved to its present form to meet those very needs. But masses of isolated, ignorant peasants are no longer the problem.

What Is Happening Now?

Two things. The clerical cord is drying up, and the baby is growing up. Few enter seminaries; not enough stay to replace those who die, retire, or resign. The median age continues to rise as the numbers drop, and there is no requirement of continuing education. So communities wait for someone to be sent out to "do eucharist" for them, and the man who comes may be decades behind their own vision of church.

On the other hand, more and more communities are finding within themselves the vision, the commitment to real ministry, and even the leadership and theological understanding that used to have to come from outside. They are coming of age as Christians and as communities: seeing the needs around them and working together to minister to those needs. They are not afraid to articulate their faith and are aware of their own need to celebrate eucharist as a community regularly. But whether they actually do it depends on the availability of a member of the diminishing core of clergy; and if one comes, will he enter into all that *they* have to celebrate or just walk-through a dry ritual?

Picture a group of Christian couples who share their talents in an ongoing effort for marriage enrichment and support. They have borne each other through difficult times and have nourished each other with love and encouragement. They find it natural to bake a cake and put on a pot of coffee when they gather; eating together signs family. What if that sign of union came to also include a moment of conscious recognition of Jesus in their midst, of the passover they make together?

There is no doubt that Jesus *is* with them—"whenever two or three of you are gathered in my name," or that they would *naturally* break bread when they gathered—like the fishermen on Friday nights and the three travelers at Emmaus. Is there any doubt that they *should* celebrate eucharist? We are looking at the very same set of circumstances that generated first-century eucharists—"and when you do this, do this in memory of me."

We are a generation at the same evolutionary crossroads as the first-century Christian communities, and we are stuck here until we can decide what we really mean by the "power" to do eucharist.

When one understands the dynamics of a vibrant community, does it make any sense that its celebration of the Lord's passover supper be "hosted" by a stranger whose only contact with them is as professional presider? If Grandpa can't be there to carve the turkey, do we call in "Manpower"?

What Are the Choices?

Choices will vary from one community to another. A congregation that is content with a more passive role—to be there for the weekly hour of worship and an occasional social function—will probably also continue to be content with a leader from "Manpower"—as long as it can get one. Even some more active congregations—if their assigned leaders have become one of them—will not experience the crisis that provokes the question.

But what happens when the child *is* strong enough to breathe and eat independently, and the cord no longer *can* provide enough nourishment? Those communities are forced to make a choice. Are they willing to do without eucharist or not?

Can they, or we, continue to accept the major premise on which this whole dilemma rests—that the value of a male celibate clergy and the limitation of the role of presider to that group alone is *more important* than the regular, full, intimate celebration of eucharist by a community who live together and minister together and incarnate Christ in their world?!

The moment of birth is precipitated by need—survival! If a child could decide to stay in the womb, it would die. Christian community life *demands* eucharist, regularly, flowing out of who they are and what they do. And what makes eucharist happen: saying words over bread, or living the gospel life together in community so deeply that it makes eucharist a way of life? For some communities experiencing this crisis, the only way out is birth.

Then Who Presides?

If eucharist flows from the life and ministry of a Spirit-filled community, then the choice of presider—"facilitator" is better —flows from the inner dynamic of that community. Of the many gifts that are present in the members, some have the gift of being able to help us join with Jesus present in his thanksgiving and his passover journey. There may be one—or many —who have that gift within and in relation to a given community; they will be sought out and called on to use that gift.

For Everything Its Season

Times change, perspectives shift. What one generation deems its best effort to protect and hand on the gospel can outlive its usefulness and become a burden and an obstacle. It is the responsibility of every generation to measure tradition as it has received it, and its living of the gospel, against the original yardstick.

It is the faith of the community, in the tradition of those common people who were the first circle of twelve, that *is* the locus of Jesus' presence and makes the sharing of bread a eucharist—their faith and the Spirit of God "who blows where it will."

There are communities that have already gone on record as having eucharist—regularly—with one or other of their own as lead celebrant (Schillebeeckx, *The Right of the Community to a Priest*). Others have done so quietly, without public statement, like the woman in chapter 4, above. Still others have thought it through, talked it over. More will follow.

There have been times of transition before, periods of measuring growth and making decisions. We can continue to baby a child into adulthood, but there are healthier, more egalitarian terms to which that relationship should move. Communities that have matured in vision and service and prayer will see Jesus in their gatherings. They will come to see eucharist as their own, first as a need and then as a must. Some communities may never take the step, but for those who do, there will be no doubt. Like the disciples at Emmaus, they will recognize who is with them in the breaking of the bread.

Discussion Questions

1. "When one understands the dynamics of a vibrant community, does it make any sense that celebration of the Lord's passover supper be 'hosted' by a stranger whose only contact with them is as professional presider?" What do you think?

2. As the number of clergy diminishes, more parishes will be told a priest will visit them only once a month. If that were

to happen to your parish, would you meet only when he comes? Meet on Sundays and pray without breaking bread? Meet on Sundays and pray and share bread you saved from a few weeks ago? Ask one of your community to lead you in eucharist?

10

Eucharist without Clergy

Reducing the matter to its simplest terms, one might say that, as the Italian bishops see things, God gives the bishops the power to transmit both the grace and the ministries to the people; according to the mind of the people of the community, the Lord gives the grace and the Gospel to the People of God and the latter creates for itself the historical forms which the ministries and sacraments take. (Giovanni Grazoni, "An Account of Experiences in Italy," in The Right of the Community to a Priest, *E. Schillebeeckx and J. Metz, eds. [New York:* Concilium, Seabury, 1980], *p. 18)*

If liturgy is to come to life for [many of our generation], no amount of revising our services will make the difference. It is a question of starting not from liturgy but from life, and helping them to see . . . it has to do with social action, with the use of matter, with life in community— with how, in fact, the common can be made holy. The trouble is that [liturgy] has lost its living roots in the soil of the world and become a pot-plant in the sanctuary of the Church. Even for most church people, I doubt if the scales can fall from their eyes until they see it growing naturally again—out of the ordinary sharing of ordinary life, as in the cottage at Emmaus. (John A. T. Robinson, The New Reformation? *[Philadelphia: Westminster Press, 1965],pp. 83–84)*

The Spring Hill Experience

My husband and I attended Spring Hill College in Mobile, Alabama, in the late 1960s and were blessed to be part of a group of students who shared an extraordinary experience of church. There was a real sense of community and mutual support. Various ministry groups worked locally; one group spent summers working in a Mexican village. Our liturgies really summed up and celebrated our lives in the Spirit. We knew what it was to be church from that community.

When we left college and returned to parish life, it was very difficult to find *any* parish that pursued that kind of warm community and outreach ministry. Where we settled in the Midwest, the old farm families had had a high level of parish involvement at one time, and certainly knew how to take care of each other. But they had given up fighting an autocratic pastor and worked quietly among their own. What newcomers saw—the public side of the parish—was lifeless liturgy and little evidence of any activity. So we, like many of our college classmates scattered across the country, spent our first years of parish life trying to re-create our "Spring Hill experience."

We started working in the system—youth ministry, an adult group, confirmation—trying to convince ourselves that we could "love our pastor into" a more mutual experience of church. He was invited to all the family celebrations and the children's birthday suppers, but he had no room in his mind for "lay" involvement in church—signs of peace in Sunday worship, holding candles during Easter vigil, women readers of scripture (he said he did not know any who had the ability!), the adult discussion group, any kind of parish council. Working in the parish was difficult and futile, like Sisyphus pushing the rock up the hill only to have it roll back down, time and time again.

Classmates of ours, who had married and moved to the Pacific Northwest for graduate studies, took another approach.

They wrote to us in the early 1970s that they had given up any hope that organized Catholicism would ever become *church*, and so had begun to gather with other families in homes to nurture and pray and celebrate eucharist.

Their announcement took me completely by surprise. Their leaving the institution, even two thousand miles away, made me feel so much more alone in the struggle. I felt threatened by the news of their decision.

Five years went by. We decided that providing our two little girls with negative experiences of church, footnoted with stories of the golden past, was not the way to share the good news with them. We began going to another parish, got involved in a ministry not dependent on parish staff, and found small groups in and out of parish for support. We were looking for options.

I called our college friends in the early 1980s. I needed to know about their journey with church; I was *ready* to know. They told me that when they started their family, they continued to gather in a household church because they felt that their children were not really welcomed in the parish assembly. The members of the community nourished each other, welcomed their children to belong and serve with them, baptized their babies. The experience was positive, and it was encouraging to hear that there was life beyond what we had tried.

They liked the idea of belonging to a household church. It had worked well while they were in the Northwest, but when they finished grad school and moved to a different state, they found it difficult to find or re-create such a network. At the time of that conversation, they were looking at local parishes.

Our friends were pioneers. I had known many people who were dissatisfied with the lifelessness of institutional assemblies, but all of them had either put up with it, joined another denomination, or dropped out completely. This couple's experience was the first I had heard where people created their own alternative forms of community. I know now they were not alone.

The Time Was Right

The period before and during the Vatican Council was a time for theological catch-up. The myths and mystique of priesthood and eucharist we had known as children were re-examined, and a theology of sacrament emerged that gave more attention to Jesus' presence among us *all* the time, that saw eucharist as the thanksgiving prayer of a whole *community*, not just the work of one person.

Because of the excitement of the spirit of the council, the 1960s saw the swelling of the number of candidates in seminaries and convents. When the council statements repeated the early church understanding that *all* the baptized are called to Christian service, the tide changed. In the late 1960s and early 1970s the movement was *out* of convents and seminaries and *into* the Peace Corps and schools of theology.

In retrospect, I can see that our group at Spring Hill was part of that larger movement. The friends who took the next step, who began a household church, were part of something larger too.

Other household communities were gathering in the early 1970s. Most of the early groups that I have heard about were made up of graduate students, not just in theology but in various fields, people who were confident of their own understanding and brought that confidence to matters theological. It "made sense" to them that the small community that worked together, prayed together, should also share eucharist together, without hiring an outside leader. Some groups were started by women who not only shared a community consciousness, but had decided it was time to step over Rome's male-only policy of liturgical leadership.

Community-based eucharist continues. Celebrations flow naturally from the spirituality of community members, who are one with each other and with the spirit of Jesus, and who find it most appropriate to express that unity in eucharist.

What follows is a collection of stories of people from all over the country. They do experience or have experienced Jesus in the breaking of the bread within small, home-based communities, with no Rome-certified presider. Neither the names nor the specific locations of these groups will be given: they are flourishing quietly, unnoticed.

Bread Communities

A member of a religious community remembered her first experience breaking bread with about ten other sisters "back some years ago."

> "It was a typical eucharist. We read the assigned readings of the day. With the eucharistic prayer we each took a paragraph. According to convention, maybe, there should be a single person who says the whole eucharistic prayer, but we felt we should do it this way. Whoever's turn it was when we got to the prayer of consecration said it."

She said that male clerics who had presided at eucharist for the sisters had started the practice of having everyone present read part of the eucharistic prayer. "They passed the Canon around, so it wasn't a great transition of consciousness to realize we could do it ourselves without them."

Theology graduate students in the Midwest were gathering regularly for supper and sharing. These evenings were not just for academic discussion, but for personal sharing, bonding, and mutual support of a group of very committed persons. The students decided it would be appropriate to celebrate eucharist at these suppers. They take turns writing prayers of thanksgiving for these meals that are consciously eucharistic. They share scripture, break bread, and pass around a cup of wine. To avoid conflict with official policy, they do not name what they are doing, but they have no doubt about the "validity" of their action.

A woman "out East" said she used to belong to a group that broke bread:

> Everyone participated. It was very powerful. It was entirely different than an ordinary liturgy would be. We sat in a circle, with the loaf of bread and cup of wine in the middle. The idea was of the community gathered. We did all the prayers—the confession of sins and everything. We were concerned with the oppression of women, racism, injustice in the world.
>
> We had a discussion of the scripture readings, then the liturgy of the eucharist and the bread was broken. No special person did it—whoever wanted to did it. Bread was composed of many grains—we made ourselves one with all of creation, like the creation theology Matt Fox talks about. The cup was the blood of the new covenant. If I take the cup it signifies that, yes, I am part of this.

A couple in the Midwest—he was ordained a priest before he was married—celebrates eucharist with their families when they go home on visits:

> I don't think they would have thought to do it if we hadn't suggested it, but no one of us has more power—we *all* do it. They've all talked about how much it means to them to pray together this way. One doesn't go to church anymore, but he really likes this. We all care for each other—he wishes church were like this.

One woman gave me a history of groups she has belonged to, in the East and Midwest, that have broken bread together:

> In the mid '70s there was a women's group [in the East]. We were all friends, all grad students. We read scripture. It naturally led into discussions on why it should be necessary to import a foreign person if we wanted to do more, so we broke bread. There was no formal prayer: we broke with the Canon, but it was scriptural.

After six months she moved away. She became part of another group—women working at a university, "a support group that included spiritual needs. Bread and wine were included as part of a meal. Sometimes we got together and talked; other times we shared scripture. For me, it filled a real need."

After another move, she found a third group. "Elderly radical nuns and grad students" asked her to join. "They were all women, all Catholic. I don't know of any men who've done this. We were working out personal issues—the line between personal support and prayer is blurred."

A Midwesterner said that she has broken bread with small gatherings that are part of nationwide movements:

It is not the majority [of Catholics], certainly, but there are movements. They have a meal, share their own stories, some scripture, talk about what their being together means in terms of God—the God experience in their lives.

She said she likes to ask others to see church beyond institution:

What kind of celebrations do you do that say you are one, and you are with Jesus? When I am with a group that's really sharing their heartfelt needs, understandings, concerns, something happens in that group that is of us but *not* of us—God?—my concept of God is much broader now.

A woman in the Southwest told me she meets with a group of women one evening a month for prayer and mutual support:

We don't do any formal "churchy stuff," but we share a simple meal. Sometimes we read scripture, sometimes we have a reflection, and we break bread and share the cup. We do it because this is what Jesus did, and he asked us to do this in his memory.

We don't call it anything. I think some people would have a hard time with that if we did. But others of us are sure: this is eucharist for us—we know the Lord is present.

She said her first experience of community-based eucharist was seventeen years earlier in New England. She and her husband were active in a marriage encounter community, and they would celebrate eucharist at some of their gatherings. "The idea came from a former priest: why don't we do it? So we all did. No one thought that he had the power—we all did."

In the mid-Atlantic region, a university community had a number of table fellowships, each meeting in homes to pray and share bread and wine. "Some didn't want to call it eucharist; some were sure it was."

A woman who does spiritual direction in the rural Midwest told me about a farm couple who came some miles to spend a weekend with her. Because they were away from their own parish, she asked them what kind of church they wanted to attend—quiet? active? They said they wanted to pray with her:

> When they arrived Sunday morning, we sat at the kitchen table and started talking about reconciliation. That was important for them at that time. We talked for the longest time—hours. Finally I suggested that since we had been here a long while and had finished our reconciliation, we might move into the living room to continue.
>
> We brought bread and wine into the living room. Eucharist is about giving thanks and remembering, so we remembered each of the people we were thankful for. We kept going in a circle, the three of us, and remembering all those who helped us to remember Jesus' presence. I don't want to imitate the Roman Catholic liturgy, but to do what's natural—use the gospel, our own theological reflection.

Volunteers staffing a shelter for the homeless used to go to a nearby parish for Sunday worship, "but we haven't been there for a while. Now we celebrate here [at the shelter] every Friday night. Everyone staying here is invited. We pray. We break bread. I don't know what you choose to call it, but *we* know what it is."

A women's group gathers for worship every week at sites that rotate throughout their city area:

> Last week, eleven of us were there at the apartment. We talked for a while. Then we read a few selections from scripture. We shared experiences we had had during the last week. There was an awareness that we are all equal before God. One woman led us in remembering Jesus' life and his last supper. We broke bread, passed around a cup of wine. There was a feeling of peace and togetherness.

In October 1987 three thousand women gathered in Cincinnati for "Women-Church: Claiming our Power." The women's celebration of eucharist was a major focus of the three-day conference:

> The day started with a prayer to consecrate *us* [to God's service]; then we kneaded the bread together, using flours of various colors to show our unity. That evening, we all gathered for eucharist. We shared a ritual of sipping water in anticipation of what was to come. We prayed and gave thanks and broke the bread. We were going to say something as we shared the bread, but when the time came we broke bread in silence—it was too moving. We had a ceremony to honor the wine, and then we shared it.

Twenty-six women's organizations from throughout the United States belong to the Women-Church Convergence, which sponsored the conference.

> By this time they had reached the village to which they were going, and he made as if to continue on his journey, but they

pressed him: "Stay with us, for evening draws on, and the day is almost over." So he went in to stay with them. And when he had sat down with them at the table, he took bread and said the blessing; he broke the bread, and offered it to them. Then their eyes were opened, and they recognized him; and he vanished from their sight. They said to one another, "Did we not feel our hearts on fire as he talked with us on the road and explained the scriptures to us?"

Without a moment's delay they set out and returned to Jerusalem. There they found the Eleven and the rest of the company assembled, who were saying, "It is true: the Lord has risen; he has appeared to Simon." Then they gave their account of the events of their journey and told them how he had been recognized by them at the breaking of bread. (Luke 24:28–35)

Discussion Questions

1. "What kinds of celebrations do you do that say you are one, and you are with Jesus?" Describe one experience of community sharing where you felt particularly close to the others present and to God.

2. Do you think everyone at public worship on Sunday morning would explain what is happening in the same way? Does that matter? To whom?

3. If you have some story of your own to add to the stories told in this chapter, share that experience with the group.

11

Appropriate Nourishment

The people, they say, need supervision, control, orientation—presupposing, of course, that the people know nothing, that they are still minors and need guardians, that the laity lack the necessary orientation, and that priests will have to be present in these community cells on a daily basis in order to preserve orthodoxy. Here we may see the corruption of the elite, or the intelligentsia, for whom democracy and wisdom are mutually exclusive. (Leonardo Boff, Ecclesiogenesis [Maryknoll, NY: Orbis, 1986], p.39)

It should be clear from watching the growth and development and rebirth of church that this is a process of *conversion* by whole communities and, necessarily, by each individual within those communities. Gradually people set aside old expectations of goods and services they will receive, and instead become a member of a caring and ministering family.

Chapter 5, above, suggested how one might plant seeds of life, so that a group of people might undergo that conversion to a new/old experience of church. Chapter 6 presents a model any community might use to facilitate the next step of that conversion: shifting gears from talk to action. Neighborhood needs are identified and all members are invited to commit their gifts to serving those needs.

As this birthing occurs, there is a fundamental change in the roles within the Christian community. Generally less is handed to "staff" and more done by individuals and subgroups within the community. There is a radical shift from "priests" back to a priestly people (chapters 7 to 10). The continuation of this kind of church depends less on hired professionals and more on an unending supply of converted—committed and active—members.

Our grandparents could not have predicted, fifty years ago, the turns society has taken to get to where we are now. Indications are that future ministries—future forms of church itself—are evolving beyond those we have experienced. The emerging communities are smaller, simpler, nonbureaucratic. They are not tied to form or rubric, but are more fluid in their response to the Spirit within and the needs without. They are doing, in the home and the marketplace, what is at the heart of the gospel.

Institutional demographers/sociologists who see change coming, have not grasped the radical nature of that change; they see it only in terms of numbers and spaces. They note the diminishing number of clergy. They cite the lists of currently known jobs that will need to be filled. And in order to maintain the clerical model of church, the institution is inventing a host of new programs to process and certify "priestlike" persons who will operate under and extend the influence of the waning number of clergymen.

Most current programs are trying to prepare people for the future by working out of the outdated models of our past.

New Wineskins

Our vocabulary betrays us. A man, concerned about a lump under the skin, goes to the doctor. The doctor says, "What do you suppose we ought to do about that?" Surprised and indignant, the man snaps back: "What do you mean?! Don't ask me; I'm just a layman! You're the doctor!"

If we are serious about birthing church, our working vocabulary must change. "Lay person"—the untrained and uninterested—has to go. It dilutes the conversion and commitment of baptism until hardly a shade of ministry remains. It is time our commitment and our energies begin to put meaning back into the name "Christian."

"Ministry" needs to be reclaimed, and used—primarily—to describe what Christian persons do when they use their gifts to serve the needs of others around them. This means seeing the issues of limited "ownership" and "power" and consciously stepping over them.

Giving birth to living church means calling parish or diocesan administration just that—"administration." Keeping records may be someone's ministry, but it surely is not the prime example of Christian service.

It means doing more than giving lip service to the "good work of lay people in the marketplace." It means shifting the very *focus of ministry* from the in-house duties that serve and preserve the institution (Why does there always seem to be a photographer there from the diocesan newspaper?) to the unseen and unsung care that is given in the street and the workplace everyday. It means trading in the mental image of special garb that says "Respect me" for the image of rolled-up sleeves and the gift of time-and-self that say "I care."

Once we really think through and make these changes in our working vocabulary, we will begin to see better the frightening rigidity of the expression "formation for ministry."

"Formation" . . . for "Power"

"Formation for ministry" is based on a model of seminary "formation" that preceded "empowerment for" ritual or administrative duties. It assumes that there is, at least in someone's mind, a model of the perfectly formed cleric: docile and trained to perform the well-known duties of running a parish.

"Formation for 'lay' ministry" also follows the seminary process. Applicants are screened for traits that are useful to any large institution: willingness to put "the party" first, unquestioning obedience to superiors, a desire to sacrifice individuality for the privilege of being one of the elite. (To be made a bishop, I am told, one must "find a way" to answer a questionnaire about Vatican policies so that one *appears* to support those policies. Candidates in lay ministry formation programs do similar handstands to appear to conform.)

Certain individuals—those who are accepted—then begin their period of "formation." They will be trained in the skills and the attitudes that "the formation team" has decided "good lay ministers" should have. The whole program perpetuates a very narrow view of church and of ministry, and limits training skills to those needs the team can envision. If students sense another direction, if they deviate from or question the regimen, they are considered poor risks for further "formation" and are dismissed from the program.

Underlying the whole approach is the issue of "power": those who have it decide very cautiously on the few with whom they will share it. Those few—the ones who are "formed"—are then "certified" to exercise a share of power in some parish for as long as they keep within the limits of that pastor's vision.

Setting the Table

Once we take seriously that all baptized persons are called to use their gifts in ministry, we must devise more open and flexible forms of educational nourishment—not to give them status, but to give them strength and support. We need to set the table with a variety of nutritious offerings and let diners choose whatever dishes they need to satisfy their hunger. Setting the table, we found, can have its own difficulties, but it can be done.

The idea for a center to nourish people for ministry was a natural next step as our community concluded shared ministry (see chapter 6). We talked about possibilities. The diocese has its major seminary nearby. The diminishing number of local students is bolstered by an influx from other cities, cities that closed their seminaries rather than admit "lay" students. Still, the students were "rattling around" grounds that once held hundreds, the library was often empty, some buildings were no longer used at all. But it was still the Holy of Holies; the no-trespassing policy was enforced. I asked to use a room there.

Over the next three months, I must have talked to everyone in the diocese involved in any way with "ministry formation." They talked programs, conditions for entry (including one's pastor's permission), years of commitment, parish obligations. There was nothing like what we were looking for: classes offered a la carte, readily available and inexpensive, with no strings attached.

I talked to seminary profs about including local people in seminary classes. One said they could not *possibly* teach scripture to seminarians *and* lay people in the same class. But I have taken theology classes, both graduate and undergraduate, with seminarians, even some where *all* the other students were seminarians; it made no difference. They just edited their jokes. Since then, I have taught classes that included seminarians; the gospel is the same. Still, *we* were the hungry ones, so *we* would do the work; *we* would find our own qualified teachers. May we use a room?

All we were asking for was a place—so that people could be nourished with scripture, history, and confidence. We would supply the labor; all it would cost them was a light bulb. The answer was "no."

There is a growing consensus across the country about situations like this. More and more are saying, "Don't ask permission. Don't ask for financial assistance either. Just do what needs to be done."

We discovered that it *is* possible for any group of people to "set the table" using local talent, and to offer it at minimal cost to anyone who is interested. One woman who taught for us has a degree in theology but chooses to stay home during the day with her young children. The apostle Paul sewed tents. One of our scripture scholars manages a store. He does his ministry— teaching—on his own time, in the evenings. The parable of the loaves and fishes applies here. Start with the piece of bread you have in your own pocket, put it in the basket, and others will add theirs.

Nourishment for Ministry

The Ministry Center of Lake County was born—and continues—with an all-volunteer staff and grassroots support. We started with one class—open to anyone of any denomination— on being church in today's world. We met in a high school. Thirty-four people signed up. After all the struggles and delays in getting started, the experience of actually being together, learning and growing, was exhilarating.

Workshops were added to the classes to provide nourishment on particular ministries, from parenting to care of the sick. These meet for shorter periods (six weeknights, or two Saturdays) at local houses of worship, park district facilities, wherever.

Two years ago we started "loaves and fishes": Friday evening gatherings where we hear a speaker and share lively discussions over soup and warm bread. Topics are chosen to build bridges in our world and local community: various religious traditions, the ongoing need for Christian reformation, the ministries and insights of fellow Lake Countians. More people from around the county were coming together for input and mutual support. Still, it was not enough.

Most people's ministries are done in the context of their homes and jobs. The greatest need for support and a sense of God's presence is not during leisure hours, but as close as possible to the hours and environs of our work. We need to remember in the midst of our labors that what we do and the people we meet are the context of our own call to ministry.

Last year, three groups were started to meet that need. Two of the groups meet every other week at a local coffee shop for breakfast before work. The third, a group of young mothers, meets every other week in a home. We share what we are most thankful for that week, what is happening in our lives, what is nourishing us and where we are finding God. We call them all "table talk": theological reflection and Christian fellowship. We are becoming both church and family to each other.

The Ministry Center is the kind of venture that can be undertaken anywhere, by anyone. Everything is kept simple and at a level of bare cost. We travel light.

Out of All Proportion

It is unfortunate that the lion's share of available efforts, resources, and money goes to the screening and "formation" of candidates for institutional roles. Millions of dollars were recently invested in another facility, the undergraduate seminary; but out of last year's class, only two students chose to continue on to the major seminary for the ordination program. The "lay" people who donated the money are categorically eliminated from the funded classes. The emphasis is still on shaping *a few* to fit an existing mold, not nourishing *the many* and letting them seek the places where they are most needed and can best serve.

The allocation of funds is out of all proportion to the needs. Millions of dollars are spent on buildings and programs to train a handful of young men. Of that handful, a yet smaller number will graduate to be made the *assigned* leaders of local communities. But the decision to spend that money on more of the same is one we have a part in: church donations are not automatically deducted like taxes.

If we really believe that to be church means that *all* of us are called to use all our gifts to continue Jesus' ministry of care, then we should see to it that there be many kinds of nourishment readily available to all—with no strings attached. Out of that kind of truly participatory community, more than enough leaders will emerge.

Those who have stopped playing the power game have a different view of the meaning of ministry and the number of potential ministers. The focus moves from the needs of an institution to the needs of the people—all of the people.

What Does "The Real Thing" Look Like?

The last thing we need for the future is to form more "leaders" in medieval molds. Even those who are dissatisfied with the formation motif, who earnestly believe there should be some other way to help people do ministry, still wait for that other way to come down, as a completely developed program decorated with diplomas and titles, from some office on high. These Cinderella expectations do not fit adult Christianity.

Remember the images commonly had of the expected messiah? He would be a soldier and a statesman, at the center of church-state politics, the elite of the elite? Remember how different Jesus was from that image, how ordinary?

And remember the story he told about the priest and Levite—on their way to a meeting perhaps?—passing by the *real* need for ministry? What distinguished the Samaritan from the priest and the Levite was his level of conscious awareness of the victim's needs and his willingness to take direct action. Awareness and willingness to act—those take first place in the story, ahead of theological expertise and title.

Models for ministers have always been unexpectedly simple and ordinary—outcasts and the officially unempowered—going along doing the Lord's work.

Sam's Way

For a while, I was discouraged because our communities were not generating programs of service. That had always been the measure of our worth as Christians—what programs we were in—and then the story of the good Samaritan hit me with another new insight.

It was precisely when Sam took time away from his *own* agenda that he gave service. It is the needs that we are likely to ignore or put off while we pursue *our own* priorities—like hurrying to meetings—that call us to give service. Our grand plans and schemes can sometimes be a trap—a substitute for real ministry. How much time do we spend at meetings *discussing* service, in relation to the amount of time we spend actually *doing* it?

The realization hit me when I was reading term papers and our son Stephen wanted me to read him a story. My first reaction was to say, "Not now, honey, I'm busy." Then it dawned on me that *he* was the person I should be noticing, and I was passing him by. The term papers waited; we read. I started to realize that if I kept looking down the road for programs, I would miss all the people along the way. And as I hear the parable, those are the very ones I am supposed to see.

One after the other, a series of events made the message of the parable inescapably clear. Our Friday-morning Table Talk group had been sharing concern for the homeless in our area. The concern had developed into greater awareness and courage, and we were discussing some kind of action. Then it came out that some of those in the group had already offered their homes to people with nowhere to stay.

One week in late February, one of my college classes was doing theological reflection on our personal experiences. The story of the good Samaritan had been chosen to shed light on those experiences. On Thursday of that week, we talked about being ready to notice those in need and to respond with some assistance. Everyone's "feelers" were on.

Friday morning the Table Talk group gathered at 6:30 at the coffee shop. When it was time to leave, a woman approached our table. I had met her a couple of times that winter—in the post office and around town—and each time she had seemed hungry for conversation, so I asked her to sit down and stayed to talk with her. As we talked, I noticed she was wearing two shirts, two jackets, a hat on her head and another in her hands. I felt a weight in the pit of my stomach. I had to ask: "Where do you live?" She said, "Do you see that bike out there?" In front of the coffee shop was a bike with something like a blanket rolled up behind the seat. "I used to sleep in my car, but someone hit it. Now it's parked at an auto shop in Wisconsin and the owner won't let me sleep in it. So I ride my bike and sleep in fields and behind bushes—wherever the cops won't find me and chase me away."

Here she was, the someone we had said we were waiting for. I asked some questions: Could she work? Yes. Doing what? Typing. She had worked for temporary secretarial services, but had not had a job in a while. I asked if she could meet me for lunch. Then I headed up the street to talk to my husband. The weather report was predicting snow for that night. There was no question in either of our minds; she would stay with us.

During the next three weeks and two days, we learned more about the issues at stake here, more about the physical and psychological needs of the homeless, more about what was— and was not—available to serve those needs than we would have learned sitting in a classroom. And we did not have to have all the answers, because of friends were willing to share their knowledge, their time and talents, their moral support. A friend at the YWCA spent an afternoon with our visitor, compiled a resumé, advised her about interviews, and alerted us to potential mental/emotional problems. A woman from Table Talk gave her a course in word processing, and tried to suggest ways to keep a job. Our family doctor reminded us that we may be dealing with mental illness, and traits that probably would not change.

At home, we had some warm moments: one of the children suggested our visitor slept so well because she knew she was loved here. We loaned her books—she read voraciously—and had some interesting discussions around the table. And then there were the rages. Periodically she would erupt into screaming denunciations of all the groups of people who "hated her": all males, all females younger than her fifty-some years, all blacks, all Hispanics, all Catholics, all of her relatives, her own community church, and on and on.

When the word-processing training was completed, the visitor began to go on job interviews. In spite of her excellent skills, there were no offers. Some agencies remembered her from other times, from jobs they had given her in the past. Some were put off by her quirks, like refusing to give her first name. We sat down with her after supper one night and searched the local paper, circling all ads for office help and for inexpensive rooms to rent (she did get checks from somewhere). The next day she did nothing. She refused to rent a room; someone might look at her belongings.

A counselor in the area advised us on the parameters of dealing with paranoia, gave us phone numbers and locations of those who could help. We had another long talk, repeated all her options, and set a date by which she would have to make some choices and take responsibility for herself.

Ours was just a stopping-off place; she is back to living in her car. We see her around town. We know we did what we could, but there is a sadness for that woman, and a grieving for our own dream of being able to "make it all better." I think my husband and I would do it again. Living with that kind of illness would be very difficult for the children, but the homeless come in all kinds.

All of us who were involved with that visitor have been changed by the experience. We see homeless people around us now whom we would probably not have noticed before. We know there are limits to what we can do; and we know there are some things we *must* do. A wider circle of concerned people has become aware of the problem, and is working toward some regional shelter. What started the process for most of us was not joining some formal program, but just noticing the needs and doing what could be done. That experience galvanized people who are aware and ready, people who will eventually make a shelter possible. The gospel speaks more loudly when one has lived in its stories.

The Care and Feeding of a Samaritan

What does it take to make a Samaritan? A startling awareness of someone else's plight and a readiness to act. How do we nurture awareness and responsiveness in a person? Stories seem to do best. Jesus' stories stayed with his hearers, helped them to notice when something similar happened to them. The gospel keeps the simple directive to serve right in front of our eyes. It allows us to walk through our town and see it as Jesus would, more conscious of those we pass on the street, those who work beside us in the shop, those we teach in school. The gospel reminds us over and over that ministry comes first, that it is worth the risk, and that one person *can* make a difference.

We can reinforce that message for each other when we share our own stories. That is why something like "table talk," or whatever you choose to call yours, is so valuable. It is an opportunity to share our stories on a regular basis. In telling them over, like the instant replay in televized sports, we can notice things we did not see the first time—how we felt before and after, how the other person felt, where we found God in an encounter with one of God's people.

And we can multiply our own encounters by the number of others who share. So many parables—of the husband or the wife, of the children, of the stranger, of dealing with the past, of having courage in the present—all tell stories of life and of God. When Jesus' original parables seem faded to us because the surface has been overexposed, we are treated to all these new parables, in the vibrant colors of real life and starring the characters of our friends. We will not forget these, and through them we will come to see the life in the original ones as well.

Networking is important. Conversations keep our awareness up. Fellowship provides emotional support for taking risks, for trying again. It helps us look back on our ministries, to come to understand them as part of an ongoing gospel. In community, we reflect together, pray together, eat and celebrate together, and keep each other ready for more.

It would be difficult to imagine front-line ministry without a supportive community. But a community that considers ministry a priority will generate a network of active colleagues, alert to notice needs and to take some kind of action. That network will provide the context from which many talents and skills for specialized ministries will emerge.

Specialized Ministries

I am proposing that the best school for ministry is the local community, if it is living up to its call. Does this suggestion reduce all ministry to generic kindness? Does it overlook the need for individuals who have been trained in theology and interpersonal skills? No, but it makes those secondary to the primary baptismal call—the call to *each* person—to reach out and care for those in need.

Given a wide call to ministry that is fundamental to Christian living, there are two possible scenarios for the development of more specialized ministries. As people begin to be recognized for contributing a particular ability to the work of the community, they should be encouraged to seek extra educational support, preferably in such a way that they can continue to serve while they are learning. It should be possible—even preferable—to study scripture, church history, developmental theology, and service skills without losing sight of the context that those ideas must enrich and challenge. Evening classes are fine for this if they are nearby, inexpensive, and limited in time spent away from the home.

The other possibility is that young people growing up in an active community, or adults making a mid-life career change, may choose a college program in theology or ministry with community-wide service in mind. But the use of their acquired skills should still depend on their ability to integrate their lives and their skills with the personalities and needs of some *particular* community after college. The Council of Chalcedon made this point fifteen centuries ago. I would not *hire* a husband, whatever his certification: relational roles can only be discovered/decided *in community.*

Putting community service first respects an old axiom I used to hear often: grace builds on nature. Where Christian ministry is concerned, the most important gifts are natural; the best training, experiential. We can build on nature and experience, and add significantly to one's ability to use those gifts, but we cannot substitute for them. The Samaritan's two gifts—the consciousness of others' needs and the internal motivation to act—are critical to Christian ministry. On the most basic level, we would have church if we had just these. And these are qualities no program can guarantee to give.

This approach also respects the integral functioning of a community. The center of the system is not a school, but the community itself. A community-based approach to training would teach anyone interested in learning, but it would *not* suppose that anyone who graduates can lead any community. That selection—before, during, or after classes—would be left to the community. One of the frequent complaints today is that our religious leaders do not lead. That does not precisely name the problem. We expect persons with *titles* to lead, when many do not have the gifts necessary for leadership. And we do not pay enough attention to the real leaders in our faith communities because they are "just carpenters" with no titles.

Jesus was acclaimed as speaking with authority, unlike the other teachers. At least *some* noticed his authority. But others, I am sure, never allowed themselves to see it. Christian ministry, even the ministry of leadership, comes simply, with bare and dusty feet.

The secret of teaching or learning ministry is *living* it. We will never project to others anything more than what we *are*. If we want to follow Jesus' invitation and notice the hurting, then those "feelers" must be operating all the time. If we want to care for the wounded, feed the hungry, it must become a way of life. If we want to enable Christians for ministry, we have to help them become aware of the surprises waiting for them along their own roads to Jericho.

To keep the center in the center as we serve, we need to feed one another with the bread of the gospel and the wine of confidence in our own gifts, so that on our journey we may recognize needs when we see them, and have the strength and courage to serve them.

We have to keep reading the prophets and the gospels and Acts. We need to be fed by the stories of others in Judeo-Christian history who, time and again, faced the same struggle —even Paul who was "formed" as a legalist before he fell off the horse—and brought a faithful people to birth out of institution. Jews and Christians *still* struggle to live the original law: love God above all else and love your neighbor as yourself.

Who is waiting for us around the next bend in the road? What will that person need? Can we predict a perfect set of ecclesiastical programs that will answer all the needs a generation from now? Will the perfect program come like a messiah, on white horse bearing a banner that reads "Glory"?

What is around the next bend in the road? Will we recognize the simple-but-difficult opportunities for ministry and be ready to act when we find them? Do we want more priests and Levites, or more Samaritans?

Discussion Questions

1. Relate one experience that brought home to you the meaning of a real faith community; the meaning of Christian/godly service.

2. Did you ever share that experience with anyone before? Did sharing that experience, then or now, help you to understand more about it? To be more aware? To be better prepared to act in another similar situation? What else might help to make you more confident?

3. "Even those who are dissatisfied with the formation motif, who earnestly believe there should be some other way to help people do ministry, still wait for that other way to come down, as a completely developed program decorated with diplomas and titles, from some office on high." What kinds of opportunities have you been waiting for? How might you begin to find or create those opportunities?

Part III
Life after Birth

We are coming from a space so small we saw no one beyond ourselves, where we were dependent and passive, part of a larger being that was mother-supplier and all that we knew of the universe. We are journeying toward a world that is so large, so diverse, that we do not even know how to imagine it. How will we be able to define our role in that world, to define new relationships with others, without re-creating the one and only system we have ever known?

If we have shared our stories in community, we know that all adults face the same task in their personal journeys. Some take refuge in the first relationship that comes along. It may not be healthy but it is comfortable: it duplicates the only system they have ever known. Some find other alternatives. A few persevere until they work out a mature interdependence with others.

We are maturing as church, traveling the same kind of uncharted territory. We can look at other evolutions—Judaism from the desert to first-century Pharisaism, or Christianity from Acts to Constantine to Trent to now—to see how easy it is to slip into comfortable, stratified, dominant-passive roles. Hopefully, that wisdom will serve us.

We will need to spend time watching, collecting, creating, practicing. Which ideas are worth trying? Which of them are true to our calling and worth repeating? Out of this open experimentation will (continually) evolve new patterns. And if we keep measuring our course against the gospel, we will not lose our way.

12

What Will Happen to "Mom"?: Clerics in a Postclerical Church

In the old way, it was safer to seclude oneself in clerical-ism, secure in the possession of all the charisms and sole dispenser of the channels of grace. In this new way, in this "family" setting, it's messier. It even means being ministered to as well as ministering—and, believe me, that is hard. (William J. Bausch, Take Heart, Father *[Mystic, Conn.: Twenty-Third Publications, 1986], p. 194)*

The recent growth and development of Christians and their communities has precipitated a moment of choice between two modes of being church: "the people of God" and "Holy Mother Church".

"Holy Mother Church" implies a parental—that is, clerical—unit exercising power and control over the dependent and passive masses. It is the mode of institutional Christianity familiar to most of us since childhood. In spite of recent changes, it is still the dominant form; but, as we have seen, it is no longer the only form.

The title "people of God" implies a community of mature individuals who are alive in faith, in touch with the presence of the Spirit in their hearts and in their communities, and committed—individually and collectively—to the kind of life and service that was Jesus' gift. It assumes co-responsibility and mutual accountability of *all*—the "parent" operates from *inside*—and requires freedom and latitude to exercise that responsibility.

This is the model closest to Jesus' teaching and to the way of life chosen by his earliest followers.

"Holy Mother Church" is a dramatic role—the portrayal of a certain dated concept of church. From the twelfth century until the present, it has been enacted almost exclusively by celibate males; but changing the cast would not change the dominating nature of the role. Now, after many seasons, the roles are being rewritten. The old play has new life, new style, the acting company is enlarged. As the rest of the roles gain depth and importance, and the overprotective character of "Mom" is retired or substantially rewritten, what becomes of a person whose career—whose whole life—is tied to that role?

Characters in the Family Drama

Let us look at the dynamics of a family. What happens to a parent when a young person comes of age? There is a choice. Either the parent acknowledges the young person's majority—and his or her own new role as supporting cast—and allows that person to act autonomously, or the parent tightens the grip, asserts a claim to the lead role, and continues trying to direct and control the offspring.

In the first instance, the younger person learns by consequences and does seek advice on occasion; the relationship moves to one of mutual respect between two adults. But I know too many cases where the second choice was made: persons over thirty-five, parents themselves, still struggle with deep resentment in the presence of those who continue to regard them as children.

As individuals and communities come of age, those who were ordained to parenthood will have to make a similar choice. This is not one story; it is several.

Saint Anywhere

Meet Bob. He is forty-two years old; he entered the seminary with a real desire to serve. Back then, it was the only place where one could be prepared for a career in Christian ministry. Those were difficult times in the seminary. The attrition rate was high as new possibilities on the "outside" opened up; many classmates left and are now married. But Bob really believed there were things he could do as a cleric that he could not do otherwise, so he asked for ordination.

In his first two parish assignments, he made a point of getting involved with the people. He spent time with them, listened, and became conversant in the things that mattered to them, worked with them and was willing to extend himself and undertake new ministries—working with the young—where *they* saw a need. He was happy in his work, but not so comfortable back at the rectory.

Bob's pastor was *Father* Novak—his own mother called him "Father." At fifty-nine, he was where he wanted to be: pastor of his *own* place, where he could run things the way he wanted, see that the people received the services they needed, answer questions, give permissions, and take care of any problems that might come to his door.

Father Novak could *not* see why Bob spent so much time with the people *after* services on Sunday. Wasn't it enough to "say Mass" for them? He criticized Bob for not maintaining the distance appropriate for his clerical rank, for questioning pastoral decisions and permitting the people to do the same, for spending too much time in homes and neighborhood hang-outs and *not* enough time on "official" parish functions. His role was that of the well-meaning but distant parent, always in control.

Those were trying years for Bob. When he felt drained, crushed between the needs he saw and his own limitations, there was no place to go to be recharged. He had little in common with Father Novak, but did not quite fit in with the family scene either. He had become a Lone Ranger, a "Super-Mom." Determination and the hope to change things kept him going.

Then Dave came on the scene. Newly ordained, he found himself in the middle of this clerical tug-of-war. As active as Bob but not as outspoken, Dave found himself avoiding the rectory. "Home" was the Jones's and McNamara's kitchens, the counter in the hospital coffee shop, the basketball court at the junior high. The way he saw it, the people did not need a Mom at all. After a year, he walked away from title and institution, and moved into an apartment across town.

Three men, three stories. Three visions of church. Now let us fast-forward the evolution of that area, and look in on them again.

Father Novak still runs *his* parish as he always did, but he notes with consternation that some of the old parishioners are not showing up anymore. On the other hand, there are some new faces—people willing to drive a few extra miles to find "religion the way it used to be." He ministers to the conservatives in the area. They are glad to have found him, and he needs them so that he can continue in the clerical role that has become his persona. In his own mind and to his people, Father Novak *is* the church.

Will he—will his type—ever change? Probably not. His expectations are tied to institution. The Jesus story he was told as a child was a clerical story: Jesus came to start the Catholic Church, he entrusted to the apostles and future bishops and priests the power and privilege of bringing him to the people, and without priests and the rites they alone could perform many would never experience God's forgiveness, Jesus' personal presence.

I remember that story, the vocation talks that were part of the rhythm of Catholic education. It stirred many to the depths of their souls—God needed them! The future Father Novak set his hand to the plow—entered minor seminary at

fourteen—and never looked back. The clerical version of the
Jesus story is a part of him, not just intellectually but emotionally and personally; it is the story he has written of his
own life.

Recently he has been hearing a new story. It says Jesus
called everyone to touch the lives of their neighbors. It says
that God needs him—yes—and also needs and invites committed women and men all around him to bring God's recon-
ciliation and presence and peace to a desperate world. He
hears the stories with his ears, but to hear with his heart would
be the death of part of himself.

So he continues doing the rituals that "the world needs" him
to do, while others move on to another kind of church. He does
not understand why people are "going astray," not coming to
novenas or parish missions; he probably prays for them. He
does not understand that *he* does not understand.

Dave—and his wife—now belong to an active base community. They started meeting to take action on community
problems, but relationships grew deeper. Now they meet regularly to talk, to pray, to minister to the needs of the neighborhood, and to keep the Christian dimension in all their
ministries. The first Sunday of every month, all the families
get together for the evening: supper and friendship, prayer
and thanksgiving, and breaking bread in Jesus' name. Together as a community, they feel, *they are*, church. This book
is about them.

That leaves Bob. Bob was given charge of a parish, and is
putting into practice all he thought about while working under
Father Novak. He calls himself "coordinator" rather than
"pastor." He is in touch, as he has always been, but now can
allow determined and energetic people to start new ministries
on their own. He expects the parish council to make decisions
and delegate responsibilities.

To Bob's way of thinking, church is the parish, all of them—
the active base communities, the many devoted and knowl-
edgable people who do, for those in their care, all he has ever

done or been able to do for those in his care. They are all church together, *as long as he is there to lead eucharist.* But when Bob looks at his friends, and when he looks in his mirror at night, he is not sure he really believes that.

Of the three persons in the parable, Bob is in the position of greatest frustration and vulnerability. Dave and Father Novak have resolved the issue, each in his own way, but Bob is living with the contradictions. He is not just making a choice, but he is being asked to make his life an existential verdict on the clerical state. He can choose to remain a cleric out of fear, pragmatism, or because the satisfaction really does outweigh the problems. Or he can follow Dave.

The first option is to be so overwhelmed by fear that one cannot make a conscious choice. The dilemma, for some of these men, seems worse than the fabled choice between the lady and the tiger. How can he choose a door, not knowing exactly what is behind it? There is a horrible fear that both are behind the *same* door: the moment he, "the last priest," embraces the woman, the tiger will devour the church and *he* will be responsible. It is paralyzing.

Those who take the pragmatic approach *would* leave, but would feel that they would lose too much by going: their job, any form of financial security, retirement care. If they have settled the issue in their minds but choose to "stay put," they may move quietly into supportive, intimate relationships. There are already more of these than anyone can guess.

The Bob in the story is currently making the third choice. He enjoys working with people, helping them to work with each other. He feels he has sufficient support from close friends to be at home and connected. He spends his energies using his own gifts in service, encouraging others to discover and use theirs, and makes no claim to a more elevated status. He is a good transition person: the parish moves toward becoming a community of co-responsible ministers. But it is a difficult balancing act for Bob.

The last few "Bobs" I met—men who had come to appreciate the fellowship and giftedness of others—also came to realize that they were not a different "clerical state," and that the intimacy they had rejected to protect that status is itself a significant asset to ministry. They opted to use their gifts in ministry without clerical title, and in some family context. They joined the Daves, and the Sarahs and Beths and Jims, who are birthing a postclerical church.

As the universal call to ministry becomes clearer, ordination to an elevated clerical state ("ontic change," or change in one's very being) makes less and less sense. We are in transition; as we watch, the commitment of the *whole* Christian family to ministry is beginning to replace "ontic difference" as the basis of intrachurch relationships. And the commissioning of particular persons for particular ministries, for finite periods of time—extending the concept of orders to the wider community through shared ministry, councils of elders, coordinators, leaders of eucharist—makes this whole process easier.

It is time to retire the role of "Mom" and go back to "but I have called you all friends."

Discussion Questions

1. Consider the three cases: Father Novak, Bob, Dave. What problems does each face?

2. Tell your own three stories of people you know in each of these situations.

3. "As the universal call to ministry becomes clearer, ordination to an elevated clerical state makes less and less sense." Do you agree?

4. What are some specific ways we might begin to recognize our common call and responsibility?

13
What about Parishes?

It is true that organization is a solution to chaos. Indeed, that is the primary reason for organization: to minimize chaos. The trouble is, however, that organization and community are also incompatible. Committees and chairpeople do not a community make. I am not implying that it is impossible for a business, church, or some other organization to have a degree of community within itself. I am not an anarchist. But an organization is able to nurture a measure of community within itself only to the extent that it is willing to risk or tolerate a certain lack of structure. As long as the goal is community-building, organization as an attempted solution to chaos is an unworkable solution. *(M. Scott Peck,* The Different Drum *[New York: Simon and Schuster, 1987], emphasis added)*

The Wrong Reason, but a Convenient Catalyst

Parish structure, as we have known it, has depended on the clergy to do the rituals and rule the assembly. However, the number of clergy candidates dropped steeply during the mass exodus from seminaries and formation houses in the late 1960s and early 1970s. Ordination classes no longer replace those retiring, dying, or leaving the system. After twenty years, the trend has become the pattern.

For some people, their sense of church and of the call of their baptism has already been urging them toward a less structured, more mutually responsible, form of church. Others who have been comfortable have not sought change, but will encounter it nonetheless. For without those numbers of clergy, some change in the governmental structure of parishes is inevitable.

This change can go either of two ways. If the priority is the vertical shape of the present structure, someone will invent new ways to maintain it with fewer clergy or admit more groups of people to clerical status. Suggestions for that kind of adjustment have been surfacing over the last few years.

If the priority is community—church as described in this book—then the parish will become the responsibility of all the members, more horizontal. Leadership will be more broadly based; our concept of ordination will undergo radical change. This is beginning in some parishes even now; the more a particular group grows toward real community, the more naturally this transition seems to occur on its own.

Stages of Community

Because this book is about community and life—small communities breaking through the rigidity and sterility of institutional religion, being born to new life—I welcomed the publication of Scott Peck's latest book with real joy. He makes the point, in a much stronger voice than my own, that it is *only* through community—commitment, mutual vulnerability, inclusivity, shared leadership, and decision by consensus—that we can begin to find the alternative to mutual self-destruction. At risk, he says, is nothing less than the survival of humankind.

Particularly significant to our question of parishes are the stages Peck identifies in the development of any community. He lists four: pseudo community, chaos, emptiness, and community.

We enter any group at the level of pseudo community: everyone is cordial, careful to overlook any differences, cautious to avoid, with polite generalities, any possible disagreement. Some of our social encounters are not expected to go beyond this: party chatter, pleasantries exchanged at the drinking fountain. Some relationships we wish *would* go beyond this: conversations at family gatherings, parish worship. Peck focuses considerable attention on church congregations, which, he laments, usually remain "pseudo communities" of polite and guarded individuals.

When we discussed these stages in one of my classes, a student remarked that she had just had a "pseudo conversation" with someone, and that the awareness of these levels has made her all the more hungry for the real thing.

The necessary next stage is an attempt to move the encounter to a deeper level by means that are instinctively chosen but actually counterproductive. Members seek to solve one another's problems or convert the others to "the *right* way" of thinking by imposing views and solutions on them. The result of this "attack" on one another is chaos, confusion, and a desperate desire for the return of security and order.

Those who give in to the panic and immediately begin to impose structure, or who look to a leader for control, or who divide into subcommittees to generate separate quiet reports, will find some relief, but will not achieve their more important goal. They will not achieve community. Instead, they will be back in the safety of pseudo community where nothing so frightening as an open clash of views and feelings is likely to occur.

To give birth to community, and therefore to church, requires that we let go of the need to control or to be controlled, that we survive the period of chaos, and that we enter into an even more difficult stage—emptiness. This stage feels like death, void; there is nothing familiar to hold onto. It lasts as long as it takes us to let go of ideas and attitudes that get in the way of really hearing each other.

We sit, alone and defensive, until we take down the walls and know that we are connected with all those others, *even with* their different views. Then, in that quiet sense of peace, community happens.

Community has to happen from the bottom, from inside. A leader can facilitate only the beginning of the process; by the end the leader will be only one of the members, who have *all* become leaders.

Community even takes priority over task. Communities that choose to continue over the long term or focus on some task, need repeated periods of emptying: to listen, to become one, so that they keep their unity centered and bring their unity to their task. This kind of vulnerable, equal, listening, and lasting community is our goal.

Base Communities

Our Christian tradition holds that both church and family are called to be covenant communities, loving and intimate networks of persons with one another and with God. Community is made of presence—personal consciousness of and attention to one another. That is why it is sad that when families gather for holidays, in an atmosphere of festivity and gaily wrapped packages, they sometimes find so little personal *presence* of one to the other. And some people are coming to realize how sad it is that, when congregations gather to celebrate the family that they are to each other and with Jesus, there is so little personal *presence* of one member to the other there either.

Both church and family have the call and certainly the potential to be present to each other, to work through all the levels of growth, and to be community to each other. It is my understanding that that call is more than a casual invitation, that it is *only* in becoming community that there is the possibility of really being family, of really *being* church.

Hunger for community accounts for the current rise of grassroots clusters called base communities. Developed in Latin America to deal with their own struggle to be *present* as church, the concept of base communities is now being warmly welcomed throughout the U.S.A. People meet in homes to build connections with each other, to pray, to read scripture, to discern how they are being called to serve their neighbors, to take action.

In their development, base communities follow Peck's pattern for the development of true community. The small familiar groups allow the opportunity to listen and be heard, to go through the chaos and the letting go, to be present to others and experience the warm conscious presence of others to us. The task, if we can call it that, is the sharing of personal experiences in the presence of God, and the discernment of direction for future ministries.

Base communities are ground-level operations. They begin with the union of members committed to one another, to forming community and doing ministry. They are primary communities, original creations; they are not carved out of something else. In base communities, there is a confidence that the Spirit moves among us; they may be networked, but they are not looking elsewhere for validity. As I have come to understand church, the base community is church in its most primary form. And the current emergence of base communities is at the heart of the birthing of church.

Is Base Community the Same as Parish?

Most parishes are far too big to allow even speaking acquaintances among all members, and so the dynamics that enable us to grow toward community cannot realistically take place. The few parishes that are small enough to permit that kind of interaction still have to choose whether or not to be that open with each other. They *may* opt for pseudo community. The rest, the larger parishes, have other choices: they can support the communities that do begin within them, or not; they can take steps to encourage the generation of new small communities within the parish, or not.

The model for the formation of parishes is the antithesis of the way community grows. Parishes are subdivisions of larger governmental structures. The whole is broken into smaller parts to make management more effective and to allow for more efficient delivery of goods and services. The system works from the top down: from the agents of the government to the governed, from the producers to the consumers.

Parish is built on a political model: a strong central city government with offices in every neighborhood—precinct workers who provide city services to residents. The city workers are the suppliers and the residents are the consumers. The parish staff are the suppliers and the parishioners are the consumers. Our understanding of church, of relationships with each other and with God, has outgrown this old political model.

The old model of parish focuses on programs and projects that keep everyone busy, often raising funds for in-parish use rather than looking beyond the fence to those in need. To be a good Christian has come to be measured by the number of parish committees one joins, and not by real service to real needs.

The inner dynamic of the parish is much different from the inner dynamic of the base community. Strong order and quiet complicity have been the parish pattern, the level of pseudo community. Seldom does parish decorum erupt into chaos. When that does happen, either someone from the diocese arrives "to restore order," or the ones involved retreat toward safety. In either case the result is the same—continued pseudo community.

Is It Possible for Parishes to Support Small Communities?

Dennis Geaney's book, *The Quest for Community: Tomorrow's Parish Today* (Notre Dame, Ind.: Ave Maria Press, 1987) gives a number of examples of parishes that *are* nurturing, parishes that are assisting the birthing process. Such parishes have consciously let go of old roles and stereotypes; there is no room for dictator or slave, enforcer or cringer. Parish policies are decided by the council; the pastor participates but does not rule. Members are more important than are structures and rules; marginal groups are welcomed. All are encouraged to use their gifts in ministry. There is room for genuine bonding, honest disagreement, and the existence of many smaller base communities.

The book includes an interview with a very centered young pastor:

> The shocker of the evening was his one-liner: "I do not see myself as a priest." . . . More important than his ordination is his baptism, which puts him on an equal footing with every parishioner and staff member. This vision makes collaborative ministry possible by striking at the roots of clericalism. (pp. 78, 79)

This kind of parish—centered in the community and not in clerical authority or diocesan offices—*can* support smaller communities. This kind of parish can provide new members, can allow for cooperative ministries, and can provide the nurturing environment for further growth.

Means of Support

A community dies without new members. It closes in on itself, experiences stagnation, and gradually dwindles in size. There has to be some source of new life. It can be difficult for interested people to find small, home-based communities. But the occasional gathering of these groups at public worship can provide an easy entry. A larger network, a parish, can help those searching to *find* a small community where they can feel at home and can use their gifts.

An open parish, meeting in council, can be a forum for discussing ministry needs of the area, and for promoting and encouraging cooperation of the various communities in meeting those needs. The particular gifts and insights of each of the constituent communities can benefit all members of the wider network.

An open, community-focused parish can provide a supportive network for smaller communities during periods of internal transition or slack. During a period of chaos, which is healthy and directed toward growth but nonetheless painful, or when a small community is struggling to refocus its original dream, the energies and commitment of other base communities can help that foundering group come to a new sense of vision and purpose.

The Role of the Parish

If true community is a priority in the birthing of church, and if most parishes cannot or do not serve that need, then it will be in some auxiliary role to the smaller communities that parishes will find their purpose. Specifically, parishes can welcome the visitor to public worship, and then help that visitor find *church*. There is a congregation near us that demonstrates that.

Willow Creek Community Church was started by a young man preaching Sunday mornings in a theater, a man who has an extraordinary gift of connecting the gospel to the real lives of real people. Gradually others got involved. Now thousands of people attend services in a huge facility every Sunday. The members have developed a balance between larger gatherings and smaller communities so that the larger clearly draws new people in, only to direct them beyond itself to the smaller groups.

We went to Willow Creek with our children and several other families for a Sunday service. What an experience! The singing was polished and uplifting, and practiced with the congregation so that all were able to join. The gospel was read and then presented as a modern parable, skilfully performed by an acting troupe. The homily was right on target: Bill Hybels certainly walks the same earth we do and has wonderful insight.

The only thing we found wanting was a sense of connectedness with the thousands of others in attendance. Clearly there was a lot going on among those who were actively involved in the liturgy, but we were an audience.

We talked to some friends who are members, and they readily pointed out that the Sunday gathering *is not church*. It is their attempt to reach out to the uncommitted, to take them by surprise and give witness that the gospel *is* relevant to their lives.

On that level they do remarkably well. Many who come had belonged to other denominations but had stopped going to services years ago because nothing was touching their lives. But what we saw was only the tip of the iceberg.

Sunday morning is only an introduction; what follows is equally remarkable. Newcomers are invited to join one of the small groups that meet during the week—Bible study groups, ministry groups of all kinds—and that is where church happens. In those small groups people study the gospel, share their stories, build community, reach out to others in need. Again, at the heart of church, is the small community.

When I was mulling over the method of that group and the phenomenal response it has generated, it helped me to clarify the issue of the place of parish in the development of church.

Many in attendance at our Sunday services feel as we did on our visit, like an audience, out of touch with any others there. Too many are never noticed, never welcomed. The few who are greeted sometimes sense ulterior motives—the buying or selling of raffle tickets, for instance. Parish *can* be the link between newcomers and communities. But the dynamic has to be genuinely toward those small communities.

It is helpful to have some kind of public gathering where members of the many small groups can share a common experience of worship, and where people who are searching can come for a taste. But a taste alone does not supply all of someone's "minimum requirements" of church. To imply that it does, is misleading. There is no community; the very anonymity of most gatherings should make that obvious.

In every parish, as at Willow Creek, there are some committed people whose only conscious involvement in church is at the parish/network level. It is their ministry to coordinate and facilitate the Sunday worship service. But what keeps that team going is the experience of gathering in each others' homes during the week to plan the liturgies and pray together; they would burn out without that experience of community.

Parishes should welcome all, but not pretend that the huge, less-than-personal Sunday gathering is all they have to offer. If "observers" are to come to be as connected and as invested as the liturgy planners are, then leaders at parish functions have to invite them further in, to the small supporting and ministering groups where a sense of community and church can be found.

What Might Get in the Way?

The direction of the development of base communities, from the grass roots, is directly opposite the top-down direction of parish-diocesan hierarchical structure. Many involved in the smaller communities have experienced a tension between the two. Some even find structural resistance to the growth of base communities. What is getting in the way?

Parishes operating under the old model consider it their prerogative to control and moderate all subgroups within them. It is preferred that all groups fall into one of the tried-and-true models, have a clerical moderator, meet in parish buildings at prescribed times, and submit reports. That kind of control gets in the way.

Because parish has a political genesis, and we have been following an institution toward community, there is a tension over the basic purpose of parish. Early attempts at solving the problem sought to combine the organizational and communitarian ends. The result is an overabundance of parish programs that organize people into committees, assign tasks or tickets, and count heads at big gatherings, but this cannot produce any more than an illusion of community. Parish staff provides the activities, parishioners provide the labor or the audience, and the system remains at the level of pseudo community. Meanwhile, the creative energies that could be going into community building are being drained. "Busy work" is getting in the way.

Conflicting sets of priorities also get in the way of community building. If communities follow Peck's whole process of development and incorporate the Christian gospel, they will come to value their equality, their shared responsibility, and their commitment to serving the needs of others. But what happens if they are tied to a parish that asserts a conflicting set of values—clerical domination, serving the structure instead of reaching out to the needy?

Much energy can be expended in this repeated collision of values with no agreed-upon method of resolution, no hope of consensus. The constant irritation claims more than its share of attention. Community gatherings are so many hours of shared anguish. There is risk of shifting the group's inner dynamic from the positive (community *for* one another, *for* service) to the negative (community *against* the "bad guys," against error). That change not only gets in the way of growth, but destroys the very life of the community.

A parish or network *can* provide a healthy balance for base communities—new members, cooperative ministries, continuity during periods of change or slack—provided that the smaller communities take priority, that the parish support the smaller communities and not drain their energies, and that the parish reflect back to the base communities the same sense of equality, the same preference for ministry those smaller groups have come to recognize as appropriate for Christians.

What Will Happen to the Buildings?

If parishes are no longer the focus, and if parish programs give way to small community meetings and neighborhood ministries, what will happen to the parish facilities? Who will contribute the funds and energies for the maintenance of the buildings? That is the same question of lifestyle that Christian individuals and families are already asking. If we really get involved in community and ministry, will we have the time and money for the things we treasured in the past?

Two factors that influenced past choices will change in the birthing process, and those changes will allow room for a new approach to the question. First, there is a shift in priorities, already noticeable in some circles, away from the consumer-parish with its large-scale programs and toward community-building and service. The second is a shift in the way decisions are made, from one man in a rectory to a consensus of the community. Allowing adult parishioners to take part in the financial decisions of their parish is long overdue, and the community is deprived of the greater wisdom of a larger body considering a decision together. Rules that have guided families for years will measure parish budgets: What do we need? What can we afford? A pattern of past investments in real estate is not, in itself, reason to keep that as a priority. As other priorities take its place, community members will find appropriate ways to use the facilities and the funds.

A Working Model

There is a Chicago-area Catholic parish that has within it a large and established base community. Seventeen years ago, a core group sought more celebratory liturgies, occasions for adults and children to participate freely and without the constraints of time that the regular Sunday schedule imposes. The pastor finally allowed them to use the parish gym.

The community depended on indigenous leadership from the beginning. The gifts of all members were utilized for all responsibilities: carpentry and homilies, work with the poor and work with children.

At first, it was difficult to find ordained presiders to celebrate with them. As the community spirit grew, one part-time presider asked to be a fully participating member. Since then, whenever the need arises, the community appoints a search committee to find another who shares their spirit, who is willing to go through a "courtship" period and become one with them. They are still using officially ordained men, but those individuals truly become members of the community.

There is structure within the community: a pastoral council, religious education team, liturgy team, finance committee, ministry teams. Community-wide gatherings are frequent; all are invited to become involved in peace and justice ministries and in joyous, familylike events. Members bake the bread for worship and even stomp grapes for the wine. Children are taught in homes, from "hands-on" experience of Christianity. The Sunday my daughter and I visited with them, a young woman was commissioned by the whole community for her new Peace Corps ministry. Other young people have gone to foreign ministries; the community fosters that spirit.

The community uses the parish gym for Sunday worship in return for occasional maintenance work on those facilities. Otherwise they meet in homes and work as an independent base community. The relationship with the parish gives them all the room they need to grow as a ministering community without the usual organizational impediments that most parishes impose.

Parishes—staff members and others who affiliate on that level—*can* support communities, but only if they turn their whole set of expectations and priorities upside down and *serve* the needs of the smaller communities. This represents an important shift in the center of gravity. Instead of the larger structure claiming supremacy, it functions as a network, at the service of the several constituent base communities, with no implications of governance.

This shift in the center of gravity presupposes that the network or parish take its set of operating values and priorities from the smaller communities: the same *sense of equality,* the same *preference for ministry* that members have come to recognize as appropriate for Christian/godly people. No longer would domination by any group be tolerated. Consensus would replace control. The needs of others in the vicinity would supercede the desire for bigger or more lavish parish facilities. Direct involvement in ministry would take precedence over fund-raising "for us" and in-house programs.

A new form of church is being born from an aging structure. If parishes are going to remain viable, they will have to face a difficult choice. Will the vertical governmental structure be preserved, or will parish be opened to new growth in an ancillary role? There may be as many answers as there are parishes.

The key to the transition is a shift in perspective. It is a mistake to expect that the parish be church for us in every respect, to give us that sense of belonging and community, to affirm our gifts and call them to service. Given today's demographics, the size of many of today's parishes, that is no longer even physically possible. Many frustrations with organized religion are born of unmet—and unmeetable—expectations. If we release parish of those demands, let it be to us what it can be, and look to base communities for the rest, then parish need no longer be the object of such dissatisfaction.

To the extent that the parish is the right arm of a governmental structure, kept in place *over* the people, to control and manage, to that extent it will fail to become community. That is not to say it will disappear, but it will not be part of the growth of living church. To the extent that parish is reshaped to support base communities, to welcome newcomers and enable them to enter further into a deeper level of belonging and service, to that extent parish will thrive and will nurture new life.

Discussion Questions

1. What stages of community have you experienced?

2. Do you have a small group with whom you share faith in some way? What stages would you still have to go through to become true community?

3. What more do you think you would have to share to be a base community?

4. Some parishes/congregations are small enough to be base communities themselves. Is yours? If it is large, does it support the growth of base communities? How? Does it get in the way? How?

14

Beyond the Confines
of the Womb

Do not stop him, for he who is not against you is on your side. (Luke 9:50)

For if this idea of theirs or its execution is of human origin, it will collapse; but if it is from God, you will never be able to put them down, and risk finding yourself at war with God. (Acts 5:38–39)

May they all be one as you, Father, are in me, and I in you. (John 17:21)

Jesus had called men and women to a giant undertaking, to the renunciation of self, to the new birth into the kingdom of love. The line of least resistance for the flagging convert was to intellectualize himself away from this plain doctrine, this stark proposition, into complicated theories and ceremonies, that would leave his essential self alone. (H. G. Wells, The Outline of History *[Garden City, NY: Garden City Books, 1920], p. 432)*

Throughout this book, a strong point has been made for seeing church in small local communities. The local base community is our covenant community: together we create a space where love and loyalty, community and intimacy, can grow. We are together in faith, common ministries, comm-union. We

have broken through patterns that were anonymous and uniform, and claimed a life that is intimate and open and at home
with idiosyncracies.

Having shifted from big institution to small community as
the primary form of church, we begin to see that there are
others who are going about the same business. We become
more open to our neighbors and the covenant communities
they have chosen.

During our years in the womb, in that protective environment where conformity was the rule and nothing from the
outside was allowed to penetrate, other religious families could
have been on another planet. Typical of life after birth is the
need to cope with a heterogeneous environment, to survive
and thrive with others in the larger world.

When we trade the womb for the less restrictive small community, we can get to know other communities as neighbors
and can comfortably recognize the beauty and wisdom of their
traditions. Eventually we may even recognize that we are related to *all* those who gather in community to live more consciously in God's presence and more generously in the service
of others.

New church is the small local community, *and* the family of
those many families.

The Vision at Joppa

The Acts of the Apostles recounts a breakthrough experience for the early Christians. While he was staying at Simon's
house in Joppa, Peter saw a great sailcloth filled with every
kind of animal. A voice bid him to make himself a meal of
the contents. He protested that he would never eat anything
"unclean." Again the voice was heard: "It is not for you to call
profane what God counts clean" (Acts 10:15).

The vision enabled Peter to minister to Cornelius, who had
been praying and seeking God, but who would have been

"unclean"—unapproachable—because he was a Roman centurion. When Peter understood the sequence of events, he was astounded: "I see now how true it is that God has no favorites, but that in every nation the man who is godfearing and does what is right is acceptable to him" (Acts 10:34–35).

We need another vision from Joppa. Imagine that we are traveling by plane across the Midwest. We can see below the farm fields of Illinois: each has a different pattern, some plowed this way and some that, all are contained and separated from each other by fences. Those on the ground are each confined to their own little area. But those of us in the plane are above the fences, not limited by the fences as those on the ground.

For generations, Christians have built fences and assigned each other to small, carefully separated plots. Followers of the one who prayed "that they all may be one" are notorious for sorting people according to rank, role, styles of celebration, or the philosophical statements we use to profess our faith. The walls seem to take on the permanence of the sacred after a while; no one dares to transgress what was "put there by God."

We've been looking at the walls so long that we've forgotten that *we* built them. So here we sit, on the ground, isolated from other good people who do things differently, trapped inside the walls of our own making.

But the voice speaks: I am not bound by your fences. The Spirit, who is the source of our inheritance in the first place, is free to move about at will. Human laws are no obstacle, nor are any barriers and restrictions people put in place. If we see the family as God does, we can make our decisions to interact much more simply.

If following the Spirit means letting go of pomp and circumstance and institutional politics to rediscover community, it also means letting go of self-righteousness and interdenominational snobbery to know the wider reaches of God's family.

The variety of gifts and ministries that were present to the early Christians are still operative among us—and among people who are *different* and people we do not even know—today. We have only to look over the fences, to take a Spirit's-eye view of God's *whole* family, to recognize that and to begin to live in that awareness.

Looking over the Fences

What does it take to live in that dimension, beyond the fences and human jurisdictions, in the reign of God? How did Jesus see life? What were his priorities in his own time? What perspectives should characterize his followers? As in every part of this process, we gain focus and clarity in the gospels.

1. Accept God as a loving parent. Jesus uses both mother and father images and many stories to try to make that point. We are forgiven, nurtured, loved. Those who heard it the first time called it good news: God *loves* you—though you did not earn it—and God loves your neighbors as well.

But the passive nature of this requirement is a paradox to many of us—it does not appeal to our rugged individualism to let go, to trust. So the message has been reshaped over the years. Some of us even remember being taught ways to *earn* points with God.

Nevertheless, letting go of the rich person's sense of control is absolutely central to the gospel. Accepting God's love as a child is the only way to know Jesus' Abba, and in that family life, our fundamental relatedness to all other persons.

2. In choosing one's path through life, care/service/ministry to others must be the north star. The gospels picture life's destination as a great reunion: Welcome home . . . for I was hungry, and you gave me to eat. How simple! How direct! Take notice, stop, share what you have—then and there.

When we are serving, we can speak to one another and understand one another in ways that transcend denominational differences. Touching, serving, healing were key to Jesus' way of reaching people. Caring service, and serving together with women and men of other traditions, is one of the best ways to begin to live beyond the fences.

3. Love one another. Connectedness has a value all its own; it is a ministry to the inner person, beyond all external needs. It is the experience of the reign of God, or better, the family of God.

As we learn to be patient enough to be truly present to someone, even for a few moments in a busy day, we create a safe space beyond the fences and create bonds between us that will keep us there.

4. See through human divisions. The tale of the good Samaritan cuts through all our excuses for *not* touching others: status, more important work, even "they're not *our* type." In fact, it was the outcast who was the example of virtue. At the heart of what Jesus asks us to do—at the level of ministry to others—there are no Jews or Greeks, slaves or masters, men or women, just children of our loving God.

If these were Jesus' priorities, the focal points of his vision, it would be wise to acknowledge our digressions and correct our course to follow them. We can use his markings and the journal of those who walked before us to find our way.

Those Who Moved out of the Womb of Legalism

Those of us who are Christians have to be careful not to suppose that the legalism Jesus confronted is a Jewish problem. Legalism is a *human* problem, common at one time or another in *every* tradition. That is what makes Jesus' story so very pertinent now.

The "church" Jesus grew up in was like the Roman Catholicism of my childhood. The center of Jewish life was the law, and the common people knew it *as it was interpreted* by a small cadre of men. The legal experts Jesus dealt with seemed particularly rigid. They decided what obligations were inferred by the law and what penalties accrued if they were broken, and they spoke "with divine authority." Contact with outsiders was to be avoided.

Law and tradition were preserved because they were to prepare for the "day of the Lord," when the whole world would acknowledge *their* God as the only God, and neighbors would live in peace with neighbors. Faithful observance of the law would hasten the day. Jesus altered that focus: he said the long-awaited day of the Lord had *already* dawned. Justice and mercy, its main characteristics, were to be given first priority, sometimes ahead of religious traditions.

Jesus did not replace one brand of religion—Judaism—with another—Christianity. He spoke in the tradition of the Jewish prophets, who urged others back to the heart of the covenant, back to love of God and love of neighbor. He saw right *through* all the institutional trappings to the family of God: the reason *behind* there being a Sabbath, the responsibility of "church business" versus responsibility to a bleeding man, pompous righteousness versus sincere humility. Like children finding pictures of animals hidden in a labyrinth, the insights Jesus shared helped others find the basics—God's love and forgiveness, the responsibility to accept, love, and care for others— too often obscured by a maze of human laws and rituals.

So how did those pious Jews who followed Jesus—who were as steeped in the ways of their ancestors as we are—ever become convinced that those venerable traditions *could* be let go? They saw that cultural isolation and dietary regulation left no room for the diversity that Jesus championed. If they welcomed Greeks or Persians to their table, or dined in the homes of those friends, they were shunned. Jesus' vision of God's family was too big to be compatible with that narrower one, so they chose to let go of the old tradition; this was the vision at Joppa.

Their religious transgressions made them unpopular at the synagogue, but that was not all that set them apart. Their political stands—pacifism and nonparticipation in some patriotic festivities—attracted too much government attention. Mainline Judaism was tolerated to some extent by Roman officials, but this "Nazarene sect" seemed to go out of its way to incur Roman wrath. Both the public and private lives of Jesus' early followers made them a liability to their Jewish communities.

Separation from Judaism was not a goal, but as their understanding grew and developed, life according to Jesus' vision no longer "fit" within the legalism of its then current practice. Strict observance of the dietary laws and the prescribed avoidance of non-Jews made less and less sense in the mixed communities that shared Jesus' vision. When continued pressure from the "old school" tightened, and life inside the old traditions became impossible, the community following Jesus' dream came to its moment of birth.

We stand with them at the same moment of choice. Various communities of Christ-followers and other godly people exist today, sharing traditions that keep their vision clear and help them share it with their children. But it is becoming clear that *church* is deeper than those traditions, more inclusive.

We stand with them at the doorstep. When we look out into the street, whom do we count as family? Can we recognize sisters and brothers if they wrap their turban a different way? Whom do we welcome to our table? Whose vision determines who will be excluded?

Venturing Out: Sharing with Other Traditions

Our neighborhood on Chicago's south side was 99 percent Roman Catholic. The *one* "outsider" I knew was a Lutheran girl who lived in the middle of our block. We all felt sorry for her because she was not Catholic and would therefore be going to hell. If that was not explicitly taught in the school, it was certainly our working understanding.

We were cautioned in school that we were *never* to enter a non-Catholic place of worship, and if we ever *had* to attend such a service, we were to remain seated throughout in silent protest to the error of their ways. I never heard the policy challenged; there are no windows in a womb.

I was first invited to leave that womb by a Lutheran pastor enrolled in a graduate theology class at Marquette. A few of us joined his congregation for worship one Sunday in 1969. It turned out to be Reformation Sunday. I was fascinated: the service was virtually identical to what I had known all my life. In the sermon, our colleague contrasted the recent Roman shift to the vernacular with his own synod's adherence to thee-and-thou English. His point was the need for reform *in every age* if we are to be true to the original message. We were devoted to the same cause. Who was going to hell?

Whom Do We Count as Family?

During the first years of our marriage, we became close friends with a Lutheran couple. I remember planning a trip to visit them after a few years' separation. My husband and I had long talks about what we would do if our visit included a Sunday and they invited us to worship with them. Our training said we dare not take communion and would have to attend a Roman service as well—God was keeping track and theirs "didn't count." It was a difficult dilemma, but as our plans were finalized, the visit ended on a Friday.

Our children pushed me further out of the womb. They wanted to attend Vacation Bible School with school friends at the local Lutheran church. By then I knew that Lutherans had a real gift for teaching scripture, so they were enrolled. I came to admire both the joy of the lessons and the joy of the teachers. The children learned with every one of their senses that God loves them. I volunteered to help pour juice—I saw myself as an outsider—but they asked me to teach the fifth and sixth grades.

When a new pastor came a couple of years later, he spoke to all of us volunteers before the summer session. With concern in his voice and a furrowed brow, he cautioned us not to spoil the children's experience by introducing certain negative ideas. I could not help but notice the ideas he mentioned were stereotypically Roman. We talked together afterward: I assured him of my admiration for their program, and he told me of his admiration of "Pope John Catholics" and of his certainty—now—that I was one of them.

Ministry is probably the single strongest factor in achieving mutual respect and a sense of family with members of other traditions. When persons are working together, side by side, to care for the needs of others, differences disappear. We are together on the level of the lived experience of faith, and find a unity that is stronger than any philosophical barriers.

Over the years, I have shared work and prayer and ice cream socials with those friends. I have shared faith and worship and communion, and have learned that God's family has room for more than one Christian tradition.

The next visit to our old friends was wonderful. They have been such dear friends, and now we are free to experience that togetherness in faith and worship as well. They live in Minnesota and we in Illinois, yet we can visit them anytime and feel at home. They grew up in a Lutheran tradition, and we have made a different journey, yet we can visit them in their community and feel at home.

There is a Jehovah's Witness who visits our home from time to time. Her tradition tends to be very exclusive in their view of things, as we had been. This woman and I have listened to each other enough to develop both a sincere respect and affection for one another. When she comes, I greet her with a hug. We talk, but we do not try to convert each other. We have different traditions, but underneath it all, we are together.

Now we have friends who are Baptists and Methodists and Episcopalians and Presbyterians and Nazarenes. Each may prefer the traditions of their own community, but are comfortably at home with one another. It seems that for those who have found the center of Christian living, the brand name ceases to be important. They have found a Spirit's-eye view from above the fences.

We also have friends who are Jewish and Hindu and Buddhist. They have helped me learn that, for those who have found the center of godly living, the brand name ceases to be divisive. We are all journeying to the same God, following different markings on different roads. We keep our focus through the people and celebrations of our own traditions, and sometimes we travel together and share what we have learned. We share a common goal and common concerns for the needs of others, and we can and do work together to minister to those needs.

Those who are part of a base community have usually let go of partisanism. Instead of competition to "own" God or to "win" converts, there is peace in experiencing God in the here-and-now, and in seeking peace and justice together. There is room for joy in diversity: joy for what others have found and real appreciation for what is theirs to share.

Faith and Religion

My husband and I have always made a distinction between faith and religion. Faith, as we see it, is that deep and intimate relationship each of us has with God. It is not intellectual assent to someone's list of rules and tenets, but relational. Religion, on the other hand, is a set of customs and traditions that supports our faith. We should be free to *choose* our community and the traditions we celebrate according to how well they support our faith in God, our love for each other, and our desire to share our experience of God with our children.

Our inner faith puts us in relationship with God, our loving parent. Our tradition is the way of Jesus. Our base community is the family that gathers in Round Lake at 9:45 on Sunday mornings; it "overlaps" with other communities of men and women who gather weekday mornings for Table Talk.

Our support system is wider yet. It is formed by members of many other communities—Christians and Jews and Hindus —like the space where many circles come together. The conscious choice to reach out and connect, to *include* rather than exclude, makes a strong statement to our children and to ourselves about God's love. Life outside the womb is beautiful.

Whom Do We Welcome to Our Table?

This kind of awareness makes it hard to justify some of the practices of the past. We hear the sadness of couples who have come together from different Christian traditions, and have been told or led to believe that they cannot share communion together. There is something punitive about this practice: it excludes for lack of orthodoxy, lack of agreement on one's philosophy of religion, a stance more typical of Jesus' critics than of Jesus himself.

We heard Ed Schroeder, of the Crossings Community in St. Louis, give a talk that clarified the issue. Intercommunion means that Christians of various denominations would respect one another's rites as "valid" worship and would be welcome to share communion with one another. He pointed out that some major denominations have reached sufficient theological consensus to permit intercommunion to begin; however, some hierarchies are not ready to concede that officially.

The question that faces the faithful now is: What kind of authorization does it take to change the pattern of celebrating eucharist? Whose feast is it? If it is Jesus' own thanksgiving feast, and his wish is "that all may be one," who are we to make it a means of division?

I am finding that those who have followed their Christianity down to its root system, under the surface and under the divisions, are finding a level where we are all one family. We who have found that level of connection are being enriched by the variety of traditions, not divided by them. And among those who have come to that realization, the practice of sharing communion together is growing.

When people share some experience of interdenominational ministry (food pantry, clothing distribution, soup kitchen), they will naturally choose to share eucharist together, no matter whose denomination is hosting the service. There has been no official pronouncement, but there is a gradual change of consciousness and with that comes a gradual change of practice.

Some "mixed" married couples are finally coming to the same realization. They share their life, share their ministries, share their faith in God. They are comfortable in their own traditions and are becoming comfortable in the traditions and the community of their spouse as well.

The new wisdom, coming from the faith-filled living of such situations, is that it is more appropriate to share communion than not.

Living the Wider Perspective

The rebirth of the original dream—in the life of each small community and the networking of the many such families—is already happening at the grass roots and will continue. Many are caught in a zealous impatience for the spread of the movement: they are ready to act *now* on the vision, and let policy catch up with the change.

Others wish to expend their energies trying to lobby for institutional change, and *then* reach out to others when they have won permission. Gestation is never uniform.

Whether this wider perspective of church will be endorsed on an institutional level in our lifetimes is not at all certain. Because it requires the letting go of both "power" and "superiority," and the collective birthing of all those still in the womb, there is no guarantee that it will *ever* happen. But when we hear the call to seek after the reign of God, we cannot sit still, looking at the fences, that wooden womb of our own making. We cannot wait for massive systematic change either, any more than could our Jewish predecessors and the Greeks and Samaritans they called family.

Discussion Questions

1. Try to put your faith relationship with God into words. In what ways does your religious tradition support your faith?

2. Have you ever worshiped with or shared with or served with people of other traditions? Tell about it. How did that experience help support your faith?

3. What specific activities might you or your community share with people of other traditions to find and build on our common ground?

15

The Catholic Womb:
Hierarchical Structure

The old Reformation was compatible with the survival of clericalism, and indeed its reassertion in fresh forms, although it [clericalism] certainly is not scriptural. The new Reformation must see it go, if the whole Body of Christ is really to be released for its ministry to the world. . . . The organs through which this theological thinking will most distinctively be done have yet to be fashioned. But the embryonic forms of them are doubtless visible in the lay institutes, the evangelical academies, the ecumenical centres, and, in much humbler but no less important ways, the listening posts of Christian presence and Christian dialogue in a predominantly postreligious world. (John A. T. Robinson, The New Reformation? *[Philadelphia: Westminster Press, 1965], pp. 57, 63)*

If we take a closer look at the wooden womb, we will recognize the hierarchical structure—a covering that provides shape, by decisions and permission, for all that is inside, and "protection" from whatever is outside. One who looks carefully at the structure can see the work of Constantine, the inscriptions of the Holy Roman Empire, the stains of the Inquisition and the Counter-Reformation. It was constructed over many centuries, and has as many political boards as religious ones.

Around the top is the barbed wire of fear: outside the church there is no salvation.

The fence of hierarchical permission keeps ideas and energies confined and controlled. Those who see it as a sacred barrier are obliged to seek permission for anything they feel called to do, to abandon any ideas for which permission is denied. The decision to give or deny permission is, after all, defined to be God's will.

A Taste of Responsibility

It was a mystery to me, for many years, that the very bishops who gathered in council in the early 1960s, who wrote of church from a perspective very daring for those times, seemed to try to take back what they said once they returned home. They said we are all the people of God, but balked when the folks back home tried to take them up on it. Why the gap?

It occurred to me recently that perhaps the rhetoric about lay involvement meant, in their minds, that more people would take responsibility for the "work of the church." Much of what they saw as necessary work was institutional rather than direct service (see Chapter 2), but dedicated volunteers were welcomed to help. I do not think they ever intended to change their rules of operation. Judging from council statements on church structure, they obviously never intended to shift their main focus from hierarchy. They would still run the show; the "people of God" would still ask permission before they did anything.

I think it took them by surprise to see that adult members of church took those documents to imply more than that, to mean that they themselves *are* church, that they have responsibility for the mission and ministries of church, and that they should contribute their creative energies as well as their physical efforts. The more seriously the baptized took their responsibilities as church, the less they wanted to go back to the old feudal system, the less they wanted to measure new ideas against old standards, the less they wanted to ask permission.

People were leaving the womb; hierarchy was losing control. Was that a sign of greater health and vitality, or a sign of the end of the world? What does birthing feel like? For some of the bishops, for some of the people, the last twenty-five years has been a period of crisis.

The Bishops' Plight

Some of the bishops, too, have experienced a great disappointment in the working out of Vatican II ideas and ideals. Power was no longer to be concentrated in a strong papacy, but shared with the bishops in world synods and national councils. They have attended more meetings, but their right of initiative was never acknowledged. The bishops are caught in the same trap we are. Can they dare to reach out to the people and issues of their area if, in doing so, they risk censure and removal from office? (See chapters 3 and 8 for more on power.) Can they share responsibility openly with the members of their dioceses, when Rome does not even trust the bishops to act without permission?

It is a mistake to lash out at each other; our energies could be used more constructively. Before the fears and frustrations of *both* sides lead us to kill each other in the womb, let us consider the alternatives. Together, we might find the way to birth.

Is "Congregational" the Ultimate Threat?

Recent attempts to return to community-based church, using each one's talents and sharing responsibilities, are seen by some as a threat to hierarchical structure and, therefore, a threat to all that is holy.

Some are concerned that shifting the center of gravity from one person at the top to many communities will destroy unity.

They are concerned that there will be a loss of doctrinal uniformity—no "one true faith" anymore, and an end of the worldwide brotherhood (the male term may be appropriate here)—the feeling of belonging to something bigger than the hometown parish. Both of these—doctrinal uniformity and worldwide fellowship—are seen as benefits that would be lost if the hierarchical system were in any way altered.

In that context, efforts to move away from a hierarchical structure toward a cooperative community are dismissed with the judgment, "sounds mighty congregational to me," as if that were the worst possible verdict and should bring an end to all further discussion. It helps to understand that the original form of the criticism was "sounds mighty Protestant to me." That is now considered to be in bad taste, so it has been edited, but the meaning is the same: anything that does not fall in line behind the hierarchical chain of command is a threat.

What is happening is that a name is being set up to represent all that threatens the structure and, thus, threatens the peace and security of those who depend on it. "Protestant" used to serve that purpose; it was used in Catholic circles to refer to those who *dared* to challenge "God's chosen leader." It does not work anymore. In light of the abuses at the time of the Reformation, and the obvious need for recentering Christian policies and practices—realities of the period completely unknown to the average Catholic until recently—the continued use of "Protestant" to designate "destructive" is unconscionable.

Today what we are seeing is a reaction to the clericalization of church. There is a sensitivity within the Catholic body that this confinement is not healthy. Some are speaking out, some are making changes, and some are frightened. Again the status quo, the pax Romana, is threatened. This time, too, the fears seek a focus. And the current name of the threat is "congregational."

In both cases, though, it is a mistake to think that the threat is external. There is a problem, an *internal* problem, that needs to be addressed, that needs to be corrected. It is always easier to pretend we need to remain strong—and unchanged —against outside threats than to admit we need to change ourselves. So we have created a false crisis—Will we "sell out" to congregationalism?—instead of facing the real question: What *is* church supposed to be about and how can we best *live* our call?

"Christian" Does Not Mean "Hierarchical"

Many of us grew up with the conviction that the only true form of church is hierarchical structure—a mighty fortress is our church. It was not always so. The original model of church was the household community. To be able to understand the difference and respond to that realization, we should be making a concerted effort to simplify, to get back to basics, but the "congregational threat" is clouding the issue. It makes it easier to avoid the point that the hierarchical structure is not part of the original Jesus movement and *not* the most important part to save.

The hierarchical structure was formed gradually, fortified with political and military power, and eventually came to be identified as essential to the Christian way of life. It is not. Modern scripture scholarship and community experiences point to other elements as more central to Christian living. We are called to move in the direction of that center as our first-century predecessors did, to take with us only what is supportive of that simple way of life, but we hesitate to change. The old fear haunts us: What will happen to us if we venture beyond the wall?

Uniformity: Not Ensured by Hierarchy

With the hierarchical system still in place, Catholics in the United States are known to hold a variety of positions on religious issues. They understand it is "company policy" that whatever the pope says about faith or morals is to be believed. That is how they were taught: few can explain the limitations of the official doctrine of infallibility. Yet two-thirds of the Roman Catholics in the United States have abandoned the "required" adherence to hierarchical authority in favor of individual freedom of conscience. Rome speaks, and American Catholics deliberate and say where they stand on the issue. Since the birth control controversy in the late 1960s, it has been recognized that "one true faith" has a number of different interpretations, that one can, in good conscience, disagree with Rome.

We are, in practice, *already* somewhere between hierarchical and congregational.

Congregational means that each small community has the right to make all faith and worship decisions for itself. Some small communities have taken their understanding of church and freedom of conscience to this extent, but that does not imply that they are operating in a vacuum. Leaving behind some politically motivated precedents may actually bring one closer to authentic Christian tradition. To the extent that Christians make decisions based on their reading of the scriptures, in the light of history and shared experience, and try to choose gospel values over political ones, there should be consensus among them on many issues and respectful dialogue on the rest.

Total doctrinal and ethical uniformity does not exist within the American Catholic population, nor within worldwide Catholic membership, in spite of the hierarchy. There is some consensus, there is some respectful dialogue, there is even some *refusal* to dialogue. There are times when Rome publishes a policy—like the role of women—made in *isolation* from and in open disagreement with large numbers of Catholic Christians.

To hang onto a hierarchical way of being church in order to preserve uniformity is folly. It does not work. And to the degree that hierarchy gets in the way of mutually respectful dialogue, it thwarts the next purpose as well.

Unity: Not Dependent on Hierarchy

Unity is not uniformity. It is a sense of connectedness, of mutual acceptance and respect, of knowing that, though we may not be identical, we share something that is important to us. To experience a sense of unity, one must focus on what we have *in common* with others.

In the past, allegiance to the hierarchy was the source of a sense of unity. We were all part of the same big organization. We could spot each other eating our cheese sandwiches on Fridays, or lining the streets to see the pope or the cardinal go by. The unity was based to large extent, too, on Italian or Mexican or Irish cultural practices. The gospel does not say, "Eat cheese on Fridays." Looking at the world from the Catholic cultural perspective, we missed seeing what we had in common with others based on shared acceptance of the gospel, on Judeo-Christian history, on principles of generosity and godly living.

Unity in Diversity

I can remember looking for a church phone number in the Lake County yellow pages. I was amazed at the number of churches listed! There were many denominations, some that sounded somewhat alike and perhaps grew from the same base, like branches of a tree. Then there were dozens of churches not listed with any denomination at all. Could there really be that many different ways of talking about God?

But then, I thought, how many different households are there in the United States? How many different ways do you suppose there are of articulating what is best of "the American way" of life? Then multiply that by the number of ways of celebrating "American" traditions.

I was brought up celebrating freedom of choice with turkey on Thanksgiving Day. I found out just last year that many Americans whose families came here from Italy celebrate the Pilgrims' feast with lasagna and ravioli. And Americans in the Southwest have big fiestas in September to celebrate freedom from Spain.

There is a common denominator there but such a variety of stories to tell and songs to sing and foods to share. And the variety will not diminish. Stories become nuanced as experience dwells on this or that aspect of the original event. Genuine celebration has to have an element of spontaneity. So much beauty would be lost if the government were to dictate *the* official version of the story, *the* day to celebrate, *the* menu for every table.

The directory of churches is beginning to speak a different message to me. Instead of saying, "See how much disagreement there is, how much *disunity* there is," it now says, "See how much *life* there is!" See how many families tell the story of God's goodness and celebrate it and try to live in a way consistent with that goodness.

I think I should rather identify "church" with that life, with those families, than with rigid uniformity. If there is a "Catholic" aspect of Christianity/church, I should rather see it in the Spirit that gives life to such diversity than in the fence within which diversity is forbidden.

Uniformity can hold sway only at the cost of life and family bonds, and for years that is what we had. We equated church with philosophical purity, with a set of totally abstract, highly refined philosophical statements about God, human nature, and principles of order.

But once people begin talking to each other, begin drawing closer together as communities of real persons, they will nuance the stories and add to the celebrations. And before you know it, *this* family will have slightly different personality from *that* family. Isn't life and family what church meant in the beginning? And there can be a beautiful unity in that.

A Stumbling Block

In an important sense, the hierarchical system has become an obstacle to the very unity we value. Christians of Central and South America are held suspect because they apply their faith to current issues. Professors who want their students to be able to make intelligent moral choices—just in case the lines to Rome are busy when they face a question—are not one with us. Women cannot be part of the brotherhood. Other denominations of Christians, who share the same gospel, who taught us to listen to parts of the gospel we were not hearing on our own, are not truly united unless they accept papal infallibility. Our Jewish friends, who can teach us so much of our common heritage and call, must not be embraced too closely unless they are willing to call their way of life obsolete. Even Catholic bishops had better be sure that the gospel they preach is in line with current party politics.

If we let go of hierarchical structure as our way of being church, we will leave behind some of the cultural trappings that went with that, some of our feeling of unity—"another mackerel snapper, eh?" On the other hand, if we let our focus shift to the mandates of the *scriptures*, we are liable to discover a new sense of unity with all those others who center their lives there.

Limitations of the Hierarchical Model

Living organisms do need structure, but not necessarily external structure. There are two common cases that require it. Developing new life, as yet too fragile to be exposed, depends on a womb or egg shell to provide protection. And many invertebrate animals, animals with no internal skeleton, develop a shell that functions as an external skeleton, providing both protection and a supportive framework. In both cases, the shell that provides the external protection also severely limits the range of mobility.

Some fear that the alternative to external (hierarchical) structure is no structure at all. Not so. Humans and other vertebrates have a different kind of structure, an internal skeleton. Each part of the body has its own set of bones, formed and connected to support the work of that limb or nest of organs. We have shape and strength and protection, but the variety of bones and the marvelous ways they are articulated permit us great freedom of movement. It is even possible to carry on different activities simultaneously.

We have lived with a shell, a fence, a wooden womb, for much of our history as church. It has "protected" us—and isolated us—from the world outside. Now we are becoming aware of how it also limits our growth and movement. Human choices built the womb; it was not God's own design. Once we see that, we have the choice—womb or spine? The history of our own bodies indicates that we cannot develop more responsive life forms until we develop internal skeletal structures, and until we leave the womb.

The hierarchical system is an anachronism, a holdover from the era of the divine right of kings: God gave the office and God told the officeholder what to do. In today's world, that kind of nonrepresentative power structure is no longer considered an acceptable model for governance. People expect to be able to participate in decisions that affect them. Nor does the system really accomplish what we would like to think it does—uniformity and unity. But it is taboo to think about an alternative.

We in the United States wonder at the English and their royalty. The electorate votes for a parliamentary government to make the laws, yet makes a great fuss over the queen. Other denominations look at Catholics with the same wonder: "the pope talks and talks, but who's listening?"

What Else Is There?

If we do come to recognize our unity with others, based on the presence of God and the searching out of God's ways, how are we to maintain that unity without a hierarchical system? What other way is there?

There is another way of connecting with others. It has been going on all around us, though many Catholics are not even aware of it and clerical/hierarchical leadership often boycotts it. And that is the council. Many godly people meet regularly in synodal or denominational or interdenominational councils, on every level from the local to the international, to discuss and debate, to share and connect. The regional meetings of many denominations are examples of this kind of cooperative unity.

Within the Catholic communion, among adults moving into more active service roles, there are a number of conferences that meet regularly, creating a wider network, working toward community, and helping keep one another focused on the message we all espouse. I belong to the National Association for Lay Ministry. To date, we are networked with the American Catholic Lay Network, the Pallotine Institute for Lay Leadership and Apostolic Research, the National Organization for the Continuing Education of Roman Catholic Clergy, the National Center for the Laity, Chicago Call to Action, the Leadership Conference of Women Religious, and the National Association of Permanent Diaconate Directors. No one tells anyone else what to do; we are working side by side. The companionship and dialogue enriches us all.

We will have to make the effort to network our own small communities with others like them, to talk to each other and be willing to listen. We are coming out of a dysfunctional, noncommunicative system, and are going to have to work at developing long-dormant skills.

The difference between hierarchical and conciliar networks is not that one has unity and one does not—there is unity and disagreement in both—but that in one all are searching together, and in the other one man's opinion is defined as right.

If we were to use a conciliar model for our church life, we would have to move toward: greater local autonomy, representative delegates in councils, and the principle of subsidiarity.

Local Autonomy

First is local autonomy: the center of gravity is in the local community, not overseas in the Vatican or in an office in the next county. We need to learn to take counsel with the Spirit in our midst, to work together, to make decisions and follow through on them, to deal with internal disputes and the multiplicity of gifts and ideas, to build strength by exercising all our members. It is the same set of skills needed for every other aspect of adult life. It requires vision and courage to begin, and a confidence in the community's right to act; for the initiative to change the center of gravity will have to come from each local community. It will not—it cannot—come from on high.

Those trying to hold onto the hierarchical structure, and to grow beyond it at the same time, are trying to be born without letting go of the umbilical cord. They are trying to get the power structure to give them permission to move beyond it, to give them permission to take their share of responsibility, to *give them permission to stop asking permission.*

Is there another approach? Yes. How does one regard the womb one has left? With respect, yes; with affection, yes. With blind obedience? That is not appropriate to adult life. I have been blessed to know a number of people who have come into the life-after-birth stage of their faith. They have started small support groups in their homes, begun to seek out and console the bereaved, shared the grief of mothers after miscarriages, helped divorced people feel included, taken their families to help at soup kitchens and shelters, learned to do therapy for

MS, used community-building skills to help small groups learn to be community, worked with the homosexual community, led others in prayer, led and shared eucharist, made a point to include parish girls in public worship, visited the sick and homebound, started in-home Bible study, undertaken ministry to adult children of alcoholics, shared insights on the gospels, helped couples with marriage problems, invited couples into marriage support groups, aided people in depression, helped others at their workplace to keep God in the center, and more, and more. And every one of these ministries was undertaken without help or permission from the hierarchical institution.

Some of the activities were suggested as possible parish work, but were rejected. The individuals each prayed, took counsel with others, and undertook the ministry they knew needed to be done.

Most of the persons described above worship with some parish community, but the hierarchical institution is not, for them, the center of Christian living. It is not their center of gravity, not their ultimate authority. It does not limit their ministries or even their worship or prayer. It is not their primary experience of church. It *is* a wider connection with others, but where they belong, where they are loved and encouraged to serve, is their primary church, and that is their small community.

Equals Meeting in Council

There needs to be more real communication; there needs to be networking. We need to seek out the connections we used to take for granted, to make a positive effort to network with, to dialogue and serve with, other small communities so that we are listening to the Spirit as they hear the Spirit as well.

We sent a delegation from our small community to worship with another similar community we had heard about. After our worship, we shared stories, priorities, dreams, and humor over coffee and coffeecake. A number of people present are involved with other Christian groups, and bring insights from those to the discussion. We need to do more of this.

Does the grassroots networking have to completely replace the present system of larger connections? The question is not how many people can come to the meetings, but where the center of gravity is. The trap of the hierarchical model is the assumption that all authority comes from the top: if the pope does not *let* the bishops speak, they cannot; if the bishops do not *allow* their people more latitude to act as church, they cannot act. The trap is that as long as all responsibility is held by one person, we all—bishops and community members alike—do not have to take responsibility ourselves:

> Whenever the roles of individuals within a group become specialized, it becomes both possible and easy for the individual to pass the moral buck to some other part of the group. In this way, not only does the individual forsake his conscience but the conscience of the group as a whole can become so fragmented and diluted as to be nonexistent. . . . The plain fact of the matter is that any group will remain inevitably potentially conscienceless and evil until such time as each and every individual holds himself or herself directly responsible for the behavior of the whole group—the organism—of which he or she is a part. We have not yet begun to arrive at that point. (M. Scott Peck, *People of the Lie* [New York: Simon & Schuster, 1983], p. 218)

The only way out of the trap is to recognize that there is an authority greater than hierarchical structure, and that we ourselves are each responsible for being church. God gives us the call, the permission, the *responsibility* to share the message of divine love—in words and in actions—so that it comes as good news to the people. The realization is both heady and humbling, both exhilarating and fearful. We have no excuse, can no longer wash our hands and say, "What can I do? My hands are tied!" We have to have enough courage to hear the call and to risk crucifixion in order to answer it.

Christianity does not fit the trickle-down theory. Jesus said, "I have called you all friends." He gave us his Spirit, his mission—all of us. A conciliar model depends on *many* people sharing responsibility. Local communities could choose to form a confederation, which might elect one of their number, female or male, to be bishop, or regional coordinator. But the object would be better cooperation, not dictation of protocol. The communities might also belong to interdenominational councils in their town or county, to share commitment to community and ministry.

The ecclesiastical offices presently in place might be effective tools to network local communities if the top-to-bottom movement were reversed. When the American bishops met in Washington after Rome had censured Charles Curran, a theologian, and Raymond Hunthausen, one of their own, they were disappointingly quiet. It was said that they could not really speak out for fear of cutting off dialogue with Rome—the dysfunctional family pattern. During the pope's 1987 visit, and later at the synod in Rome, some of the bishops did speak out with clarity and courage.

If there were commitment to a conciliar model of living church, the bishops of the Midwest might meet, or the bishops of a country, to share the faith stories, ministry needs, visions, difficulties of each one's area. That meeting would have real value if they each would speak from personal experience of their own true communities, if they allowed themselves to step beyond pseudo community with each other and allowed themselves to be vulnerable.

The problem is the same, and we are all part of it. If we do not speak openly and honestly, if we do not put building the family of God over building and preserving the dynasty of institutional religion, we are selling our birthright for a pot of stew—catered by a four-star restaurant of course—and the robes of office.

Subsidiarity

Subsidiarity is the secret to the efficient running of many large corporations. It means the president does not have to do everything. Management does not assume all the responsibilities. A job is done by the smallest unit that can handle it. In an international body of Christians, it would mean that local communities, metropolitan networks, national conferences would take the responsibility, would act with authority, to do what they need to do to live and to share the good news.

There is an important difference between business and church. The head of the business is put there by the owners, the stockholders. The head can run the business cooperatively or autocratically, as long as she (he) has that job, and the other employees work for her (him). We say we believe that we were commissioned by God to become living church, that the Spirit lives in all God's people. There is no higher authority than that.

We are reminded—more and more often lately—that salvation depends on uniformity and tight control, on staying in the womb. Those trying to grow, trying to reclaim the original dimensions of church, are finding the womb more and more cramped. Recent institutional policies seem to have been designed to narrow the space even more. Maybe someone should tell the policymakers what happens when a womb contracts.

Discussion Questions

1. Consider what it means that "the center of gravity is in the local community." List what needs your community might attend to in order to act on that principle.

2. Can you identify other small communities with whom you might network, in your denomination or some other? How might you go about arranging to spend some time with them?

3. Peck states that every individual must "hold himself or herself directly responsible for the behavior of the whole group," or the group will remain "potentially conscienceless." What are the implications of that for you as an individual church member, for your small community?

16

Birth versus Inertia: The Struggle of the Undecided

From the beginning till now the entire creation, as we know, has been groaning in one great act of giving birth; and not only creation, but all of us who possess the first-fruits of the Spirit, we too groan inwardly as we wait for our bodies to be set free. (Romans 8:22–23, Jerusalem Bible)

Scripture makes reference to a woman "whose time has come": she is in anguish, her child is born, and then she rejoices. There is an inevitability about the moment of birth that is unlike anything else I have experienced: this is it! Wondering is over, there isn't time to reconsider, even last-minute panic can't stop it. Whatever preparation you have done is all you get to do: this is it!

There is a difference when we use birthing to describe a societal phenomenon. Up to the last moment there is still a choice. It is a difficult decision, agonizingly difficult to those who see all at stake: life or *life*, life-secured or life-birthed. Though many may get to that point, and many may look down the dark passage and guess what lies beyond, most will not move.

This is inertia. Whatever is at rest will remain at rest unless some force gets it moving: that explains why so many people are so dissatisfied with their local experience of church and yet do *nothing* about it. That also explains why it is almost impossible to move a large institution: inertia increases with mass. But more to our point, whatever *is* moving will continue to move unless some outside factor of equal or greater force moves against it to stop it.

We are dealing with a kind of theological physics. The re-birth of church in its simpler, purer form requires that the *inner* force pushing toward birth be *greater than* the forces working against it.

That is the story of Pentecost. The "driving wind" and "flames of fire"—pure energy—blasted the fearful out of their hiding place and into the streets. The Spirit is energy.

I used to wonder whether the movement this book describes would manage to survive all the way to birth or would die in the womb. But in the last few years I have seen such a variety of communities and spoken with such different individuals, who have each nurtured this new life—lived with the dream, touched the possibilities, inched toward its realization—that I have found the answer to that question is already in. The time has come, the future is now, and the birthing—with all its pain and struggle and hope—is underway.

Birth is not magic—something soft and pink discovered under a cabbage leaf—it is motion, change. Remember "inertia"? All matter—including human beings—will remain at rest or in uniform motion unless acted upon by some external force. Because of inertia, we can see three groups of contemporary Christians: those who have remained at rest, those who were moving but have been stopped by an equal or greater force moving against them, and those who have found enough internal strength to overcome obstacles and continue moving.

Look at a newborn: facial features "scruntched" together, head sometimes misshapen by the trip through the birth canal. Uterine muscles push the infant out while other muscles resist—all part of the same mother. No wonder babies do not look like themselves until they recover a while! No wonder it is difficult for the mother! She must consciously relax some muscles to let others work unimpeded.

It is the same with church. Some forces have tried to kill the babe before birth, and some seem so intent on stopping birth that they are virtually attempting to sew the mother shut. The mother whom they are trying to protect is in even greater peril. Our own muscles even fight it—inner forces of doubt and fear, holding onto the warm and the known.

Some have chosen to turn their backs on insights and possibilities that once excited them, to forfeit the measure of autonomy/responsibility they had found, to shrug their shoulders at injustices they once decried—good people. It is very hard. It has always been very hard.

Two thousand years of retrospect can make choices look comic-book simple. Jesus did not walk the streets of Jerusalem saying "Give up your Judaism! Come with me: I have something better!" Jesus was a faithful Jew, and so were his friends. Judaism was their tradition, their link to the past, the wellspring of their liturgical practice. They would not have abandoned what was so much a part of them to "sign up" for something else. They "worshiped daily at the temple and broke bread in private homes" until they realized they had become so different in focus and practice that separation/birth was necessary.

They followed all the proscriptions of religious law as well as the simpler call to live in peace, justice, and service. They had a sense that the new way helped *them* understand their relationship with God more than did the old. That sense grew into a conviction, so that when the tension between old and new became open conflict, they were able to make a choice. But that choice was not without cost.

First-century Jews who were followers of Jesus came to accept as sisters and brothers some who were not children of Abraham. Their usual abhorrence for anything or anyone not

Jewish changed to accommodate those who also shared the Spirit of Jesus. It was this heterogeneous group that became their closest community of friends. The suppers shared with "Nazarenes" came to be much more supportive of a life of service than were the temple sacrifices or the laws on what was "clean."

The governing body of Judaism saw these accommodations as threats to traditional Judaism and pressured the unorthodox to return to pure practice. Some probably did conform; we do not hear of them. But those we consider our own ancestors in faith chose to step beyond the authorities and traditions of their people, in spite of the fact that friends or family would not understand, even in spite of all the talk such situations generate.

We Christians are comfortable in our certainty that what our first-century predecessors did was right; it is easy to be comfortable from our vantage point. It is easy for twentieth-century Christianity to demand conformity to medieval customs in the name of those whose most daring act was to break out of just such a conformity. We do not even see the irony.

What would *we* have done—recommit to the faith of our fathers, or seek a new understanding, a new articulation, of that faith? Would we shun the company of those officially labeled dangerous, heretical, or weigh it carefully in mind and heart before deciding? Would we choose the "safe" way, or take the risk? Both sides faced a very difficult decision; both sides deserve more credit than we give them. What would *we* have done? Until we face the pain, uncertainty, and struggle that were the cost of that birth, until we count ourselves ready to pay a similar price, we are still sacrificing sheep in Jerusalem, or selling them in Egypt.

The choice is not without parallel within the Jewish community itself. There are three major Jewish traditions in the United States today: the orthodox, the conservative, and the reformed, each different in some ways from their first-century roots. They have all faced those questions, all weighed the importance of this or that practice in keeping the focus on their covenant with God. They have all lived those decisions with courage. Faithful living demands courage.

As difficult as it was for first-century Christians, the courage of the men and women who struggled/grappled with these issues in the sixteenth century is all the more amazing. The Jesus *they* had known as children sat in kingly splendor at God's right hand, giving "power" to humans, who sold the "power" to others, who sold "salvation" to the poor. This was the "divine economy," God's plan—and damnation to the most horrible suffering awaited anyone who dared question or oppose it.

Yet they heard from some preachers of a Jesus so different, so gentle and loving, and a God so generous and forgiving, that they faced a real dilemma. Were they to stay on the safe side of the establishment and cheer the burning of these preachers as heretics? Or were they to risk letting go of what everyone said was the *only* way to heaven—the mediation of the governing body of Christendom—in order to live according to the "new" insights filtering down from scripture?

It is interesting to try to place ourselves in that dilemma. It does not work to assume we would make the same choice as did those of our own denomination, or some figure of the times whom we admire. It does not work until we realize that the sixteenth-century reformers chose to cut the ties with their own denomination when the gospel as they read it called them to go beyond their structures and their leaders.

Our generation has faced some tough decisions. The question of racial equality was finally confronted. The "right" to wage war has been seriously challenged. But most of us offered only armchair speculation when the events made television news. Life has changed because a few dared to ask if things *have* to be this way, because a few dared to live their vision. What if the few failed to take the risk? Would there still be